the global shopper

the global shopper

WHERE TO FIND THE BEST ONLINE BUYS (Sshhh!) FROM AROUND THE WORLD

the global shopper

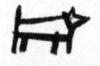

Nicole Hopkinson

Hardie Grant Books

To my nephew Harrison, who I couldn't love more if he was ordered online, bubble-wrapped and delivered to my door in a FedEx box!

Published in 2006 by
Hardie Grant Books
85 High Street
Prahran, Victoria 3181, Australia
www.hardiegrant.com.au

All rights reserved. No part of this publication may be reproduced, stored in a retrieval system or transmitted in any form by any means, electronic, mechanical, photocopying, recording or otherwise, without the prior written permission of the publishers and copyright holders.

The moral right of the author has been asserted. So has the right to shop.

Copyright text © Nicole Hopkinson 2006
Copyright illustrations © Cameron Comer 2006

Cataloguing-in-Publication Data is available from the National Library of Australia.

ISBN 1 74066 405 1

Illustrations by Cameron Comer
Cover and text design by Sharyn Raggett
Typeset by Pauline Haas, Empire Ink
Printed in Australia by McPherson's Printing Group

10 9 8 7 6 5 4 3 2 1

contents

Introduction	1
BUNDLE OF JOY Baby Clothing, Toys & Gifts	5
A KID'S WORLD Fashion, Accessories & Fun Things for the Under-12s	27
THE BEAUTY ZONE Lotions, Potions, Make-up & Fragrances	47
A WOMAN'S WARDROBE Fashion, Handbags & Other Accessories for Women	68
THE MALE ROOM Clothing & Accessories for the Men in Your Life	90
HOME SWEET HOME Homewares & Décor for Your Abode	101
WORDS AND MUSIC Books, Magazines, CDs, DVDs & More	120
THE BIG NAMES International Department Stores	136
SAY IT WITH STYLE Super Stylish Stationery, Cards & Invitations	145
SOMETHING DIFFERENT The Weird & Wonderful Goes Online	166
SECURITY AND SHIPPING Everything You Need to Know	177
Index	181
Acknowledgements	185

introduction

Have you ever dreamed of stocking your wardrobe with the much acclaimed basic Gap tees, admired an exclusive European homewares collection in an international magazine, or loved the look of some personalised stationery stocked exclusively by a Fifth Avenue boutique, but can't justify an international air ticket? Now, thanks to the internet, the purchase of these goods is merely a mouse click away.

Being geographically isolated, Australians have, in the past, often been at a disadvantage when it came to purchasing many limited edition or unusual items. Short of booking the next seat to Heathrow, we have often been forced to admire items in the pages of glossy international magazines from afar with little hope of making a purchase.

In recent years, however, Australians have discovered the excitement of e-commerce. According to Visa, in 2004 Australians spent in excess of A$6 billion on online shopping – with an average spend of A$139 per shopper.

The Global Shopper was developed as a result of much personal experience of online shopping. This has included buying everything from books to clothing and even bespoke stationery from a range of international retailers. Save for a few hiccups in my early ordering (a young friend now has five pairs of overalls in size 1 rather than a single pair in size 5), I have enjoyed hassle-free online shopping. As with non-online retailers, some are better than others, and first impressions are often a good indication of whether you should proceed to purchase from a particular store.

I have attempted to sort through the millions of sites in cyberspace to find what I consider to be some of the best sites for online shoppers. The list is obviously not exhaustive, and focuses mainly on items which, from a practical perspective, can be easily packaged and sent to Australia. The book also includes some local sites that are equally as impressive as their international counterparts. I have also endeavoured to feature sites not easily located via standard search engines, many of which are more like those hard-to-find boutiques selling only the most stylish of products and services.

Included are details on security issues for online shoppers – an area of concern for many wanting to start exploring the aisles of the global shopping mall. Much of the advice is common sense, combined with some handy hints, particularly for those new to shopping online. Information is also provided on international mail-forwarding services – a must for any Australian-based global shopper – which enables us to purchase from online retailers who do not provide international shipping to Australia.

Now it's time to shop. I hope you enjoy this book and shopping in London, New York, Paris and beyond without leaving your laptop.

SHOPPING TIPS
Here are some general tips for those interested in shopping online.

- Shop from secure sites where your data is handled by a secure server. You'll know that a site is secure when a lock or similar icon appears on your browser, usually when you get to the checkout page.

- Install and maintain appropriate security programs on your computer.

- Use the 'Favourites' feature of your internet browser to save the address of sites you may wish to visit or re-visit.

- Keep clippings of sites of interest that are mentioned in magazines or newspapers – it is amazing how time can dull your memory of exact details such as website addresses.

- If you like the range of products on a particular site, look at their 'Links' (if they have any) to other sites – often they will have products that complement merchandise from the original site.

- For overseas sites, if international shipping costs are not calculated before you check out, email the retailer to confirm the exact mailing charges.

- Always look in the 'Sale' section of sites – for fashion in particular, where reduced items usually relate to our current seasons.

- Even if a site does not promote international shipping, email and check with the retailer to see if they can send items to Australia. Small retailers, in particular, will often be happy to ship abroad but may not have a formal policy as such.

- When shopping from overseas sites, always convert the listed prices to Australian dollars to ensure you know exactly how much you are paying. A site such as www.xe.com offers easy-to-use online currency conversions.

- If you are particularly happy or unhappy with your purchases email the retailer – feedback, whether good or bad, is always helpful to merchants who never actually meet their customers in person.

UNDERSTANDING THE SIGNS
The following symbols are used in reviews throughout *The Global Shopper*:

Gift wrapping is available

The site offers shipping to Australia

A personal favourite

COUNTRY CODES
AUS Australia
NZ New Zealand
UK United Kingdom
USA United States
CAN Canada
FR France
IT Italy

WEBSITE ADDRESSES
All sites in *The Global Shopper* have been categorised into genre and listed alphabetically.

When entering the website's address, for some sites, you may need to begin with the www. spiel before entering the site name.

bundle of joy
BABY CLOTHING, TOYS & GIFTS

eat

americanapparel.net   USA

COTTON BASICS WITH A CONSCIENCE

If you want your littlest loved one to be clothed in jumpsuits sewn with stitches of social responsibility, head straight to this site. With all stages of production undertaken in a 100% sweatshop-free environment in downtown LA, American Apparel excels with a line of super-soft cotton baby tees and ribbed bodysuits in a range of colours. A comprehensive range of women's and men's clothing is also available, so if you want to combine the frivolity of fashion with an ethical edge, log on to this e-store.

GREAT FOR:
Clothing – babies, children, men, women

artebebe.com   USA

CLOTHING & TOYS WITH A LATIN TWIST

For baby gifts with a distinct Latin American flavour, look no further than Arte Bebé. Featuring a unique collection of handcrafted clothing, toys and accessories, all products are made using premium quality fabric and are either hand-knitted or hand-finished with decorative detailing. Product categories include 'Babies', 'Boys', 'Girls' and 'Toys'. For a departure from the usual farm animals, consider the woollen Lorenzo Llama or the handmade Olivier Owl from Mexico.

GREAT FOR:
Clothing, toys, décor items

babybox.com

USA

BOUTIQUE BABY GIFTS

Featuring a niche collection of baby clothes, toys and accessories, Baby Box is a premier online boutique. All products are of the highest quality, with many items not currently available in Australia. Brightly coloured woollen sweaters featuring the first letter of a baby's name and deluxe cashmere blankets are two of my favourites. Many items can be personalised, and gifts arrive in signature packaging. A gift-finder can help narrow the search for the perfect gift, and creative baby shower ideas are also provided.

GREAT FOR:
Clothing, accessories, décor items

babycz.com

USA

JUNIOR CASHMERE COLLECTION

If you don't believe that an infant's wardrobe is truly complete without at least one piece of cashmere, then this site is for you. Featuring a range of high-quality luxury clothing for babies and children up to the age of eight, Baby Cz also includes some adorable soft toys – made from cashmere of course! Cotton and linen ranges are also available, however, once you have seen the dusty pink or powder blue cashmere cable-knit sweaters, with matching cashmere pom pom hats, you'll want to go that extra retail mile.

GREAT FOR:
Clothing – babies, toddlers, children

babyoliver.com

USA

LUXURIES FOR LITTLE ONES

Baby Oliver promises 'luxuries for little ones' and in this it delivers. The site is separated into a number of departments, including 'Bedding', 'Clothing', 'Furniture' and 'Toys'. More than 20 brands are featured, including Bumblebag Designs and Little Giraffe. The 'Clothing' section includes adorable pieces such as the luxurious layette bodysuit by Tea Collection in a print inspired by a vintage Japanese textile. The 'Bedding' range includes brightly coloured fleece-appliquéd blankets and Rachel Ashwell Shabby Chic baby bedding. Personalised artwork is also available.

GREAT FOR:
Clothing, books, furniture, toys

babysgotstyle.com.au

AUS

WHERE STYLISH LITTLE PEOPLE SHOP

Aptly described as the home of stylish little gifts for stylish little people, Baby's Got Style is a favourite among many a yummy mummy. Incorporating a unique range of baby clothing, toys and accessories, the site features more than 25 international brands. My current favourites include delicious screen-printed cotton tanks from blablabla and the locally designed XO kiss hug range, apparently a favourite with supermodel Elle McPherson. All gifts are presented in signature Baby's Got Style cloth carry bags.

GREAT FOR:
Clothing, toys, books

babystar.com

USA

BRIGHT & BOLD DESIGNER BLANKETS

Selling what it describes as 'baby products for the design savvy parent and the texture loving child', Baby Star offers an impressive collection of baby blankets, throws, bibs and tees. Blankets feature bright contemporary designs including 'Lavish' and 'Yum Yum'. White cotton tee designs include a raised stitched star and fun pink and turquoise cupcakes, complete with a red cherry on top.

GREAT FOR:
Blankets, clothing

babystitch.com.au

AUS

PERSONALISED EMBROIDERED GIFTS

Trust two mums to recognise the appeal of personalised baby gifts. This site features a collection including towels, bathrobes, bibs and bodysuits, all embroidered with your chosen infant's name or initials. Clothing is available from size 000-1. A great alternative to flowers or chocolates for the new bub, personalised baby hampers are also available. The business is 100% Australian-owned.

GREAT FOR:
Personalised baby gifts

babystyle.com USA

ONE-STOP STYLE SHOP

Developed by a mother searching in vain for a one-stop baby store, Babystyle is one of the most comprehensive baby-related sites on the internet. With products ranging from infant apparel to toys, nursery items and gifts, this site is particularly strong on providing high-quality, reasonably priced clothing, especially for boys, who are often overlooked in the junior fashion stakes. The gift section is conveniently separated into ages, making age-appropriate gift selections a breeze. Look out for the newborn essentials range. The site contains an excellent FAQ (frequently asked questions) section and helpful advice for first-time shoppers.

GREAT FOR:
Clothing, gear, toys, furniture

babywit.com USA

COMICAL INFANT TEES

'You may not be cool, but your baby can be' – so goes the philosophy of Baby Wit. If baby tees embossed with teddy bears and rainbows are not for your little cherub, relief is just a mouse click away. Designs are separated into categories including 'Arty Baby', 'Pop Baby' and 'Politico Baby' with such gems as 'Future Activist', 'Insomniac' and 'Caution, I Bite'. Sizes range from 3–6 months up to adult sizes in some designs. All products are made in the USA in a sweatshop free environment, while designs are hand-pressed onto fabrics using retro-style iron-on transfers.

GREAT FOR:
Clothing

beautifulboxes.com.au — AUS

A GREAT ALTERNATIVE TO THE BOUQUET

The name of this site says it all, really – beautiful gift boxes filled with beautiful clothing, toys and accessories for the newest arrival. Boxes are separated into 'Infant Boxes' (0-6 months), 'Baby Boxes' (6-18 months) and 'Mother & Baby Boxes'. Featured brands include Tea Collection Clothing and Oobi Baby cotton tees. Each box is themed. Boxes include the 'Baby Boy Ocean Box' featuring products in a combination of green and blue hues, and the 'Winter Warmers Ladybird Box' containing hand-knitted ladybird booties and a matching hat. Most products may also be purchased individually.

GREAT FOR:
Gift boxes, clothing, toys

bebeinternational.com — USA

CULTURAL DIVERSITY MEETS JUNIOR COMMERCE

Forget the word bebe, international is the overwhelming theme of this site. From a French-speaking doll to an Asian fortune blanket or Spanish building blocks, Bebe International embraces almost all cultures and traditions. Incorporating a comprehensive range of clothing, toys and room décor items, while fairly easy to navigate, the site could be a little overwhelming for a first-timer.

GREAT FOR:
Clothing, accessories, toys

bellazanderbaby.com   USA

HIP STUFF FOR BABIES & TOTS

Not sure about the name, but the products on this site are great! Well stocked with toys, décor items and stationery, Bella Zander Baby delivers in its promise to provide 'hip stuff for babies and super cool mums & dads'. Highlights include the pink polka dot 'Charlotte' bedding sets, chic baby totes and the 'Le Bubblegum' scratch 'n' sniff card sets.

GREAT FOR:
Toys, décor, stationery

blablakids.com   USA

CROCHETED PERUVIAN DELIGHTS

In the toy kingdom there are your stock standard plush animals and then there are blabla toys. Who could resist 'Sandwich', the multi-striped cat, or Leonardo the green and aqua lion. All items are hand-knitted by Peruvian artisans and evoke memories of years past. Another favourite is the veggie rattle set including a carrot, tomato and cabbage. The site also offers a selection of colourful baby/toddler clothing, blankets and bags.

GREAT FOR:
Toys, clothing, accessories, bedding

blueblankie.com

CAN

MARVELLOUS MUST HAVES FOR SMALL WONDERS

With quality merchandise, ranging from Sherpa and fleece booties to the Princess Toy Box Bench, Blue Blankie is an inspiring upscale baby boutique. Merchandise is separated into 'Accessories', 'Apparel', 'Blankets', 'Furniture', 'Gifts' and 'Toys'. Featured brands include Jack and Lily footwear and blankets by Sage Creek Naturals.

GREAT FOR:
Clothing, accessories, blankets

coolbabysheets.com

USA

BABY BEDDING WITH ATTITUDE

Cool Baby Sheets sells what it terms radical bedding for babies and toddlers. Selections can be made by choosing a fabric print or by product type, including sheets, blankets, quilts and bedding sets. Popular fabric designs include hamburgers, leopard skins and ladybugs. Oh, and don't miss the Glow in the Dark Spider Webs and the Glow in the Dark Eyes. Quilts are made extra large to enable an easy move from crib to toddler bed.

GREAT FOR:
Bedding

doodlebaby.com

USA

WHIMSICAL HAT & BLANKET DESIGNS

For hip parents in search of blankets a tad more daring than the dusty pink or baby blue variety, this is the site for you. Featuring original designs appliquéd on extra plush fleece fabric, Doodlebaby is a welcome addition to the global shopping mall. Designs include an aeroplane against a bright blue sky and an ivory fleece blanket with a sprinkling of colourful polka dots. Your child's name or initials can also be added to all designs. A range of creative hats and costumes is also available, including a 'Granny Smith' green beret with a green leaf and brown fabric stem.

GREAT FOR:
Clothing, blankets, costumes

dpam.com

FR

TRADITIONAL FRENCH APPAREL

Du Pareil au Meme, or dpam for short, sells a range of French clothing, shoes and toys for children from newborn to 14 years. Whilst the site is not the easiest to navigate, persevere and you will find some Gaelic gems. The Du Pareil au Meme Baby is definitely the leading range, designed for babies from newborn to 24 months. My last purchase from the site was an adorable 'Body Chateau' jumpsuit and 'Lapindoux', a silk-screened toy rabbit.

GREAT FOR:
Clothing, toys

eeieeioh.com.au AUS

HOME-GROWN COTTON ESSENTIALS

Featuring a simple yet functional range of cotton apparel for infants from 3–12 months, including T-shirts, leggings and singlets, Eei Eei Oh offers infant wardrobe essentials to mix and match. To complement the traditional primary colour range, a new Candy Collection has recently been introduced. All items are 100% cotton and are designed and manufactured in Australia. The site is easy to navigate and, given the modest product range, the perfect first point of entry for those new to e-commerce.

GREAT FOR:
Clothing

gagagoogoo.co.uk UK

BIG THOUGHTS FOR LITTLE PEOPLE

You're never too young to have a sense of humour, and with a collection of cotton tops and tees featuring quotes from the big screen and the greats of literature, Gagagoogoo ensures your little ones start leading the laughs early. With quips sure to make even the most sleep-deprived new parent giggle, my favourite designs include Clint's 'Go Ahead Make My Day' and 'I'm Just Crazy About Tiffanys' courtesy of Ms Hepburn. The bib sets are a great gift idea and include such gems as 'Never Eat More Than You Weigh' and Oscar Wilde's remark that 'Only Dull People are Brilliant at Breakfast'. All items are packaged in frosted plastic gift tubes.

GREAT FOR:
Clothing

honeyforthebear.com

USA

STYLISH SHOPPING FOR BABY ESSENTIALS

The proprietors of this store have established a site featuring unique clothing for babies and toddlers. Brands include Baby Bonkie, Eye Spy, Sew Happy and Tortoise Lane. Products are categorised into 'Boys', 'Girls' and 'Accessories'. A range of gift items and products for the often forgotten mum and dad is also available.

GREAT FOR:
Clothing, accessories, toys

impstore.co.uk

UK

HIP & STYLISH NEW ATTITUDES

There quickly comes a time when your beloved offspring develops strong preferences about what is and isn't fashionable, usually leading to a lingering fascination with fluorescent hues. Until that time, enjoy the stylish apparel of Imp Store. Stocking many leading designers including Fortune Tee, Mighty Politely and Trumpette, the site is separated into 'For Boys', 'For Girls', 'For Accessories', 'For Bags' and 'For Twins'. A current favourite is the 'I'm not a Baby' jumpsuit and the 'This End is Up' jumpsuit.

GREAT FOR:
Clothing, accessories, baby bags

jacadiusa.com

USA/FR

PREMIER PARISIAN CHIC

This US shopping site for the acclaimed French brand Jacadi will restore any doubts you may have about investing in traditional-style apparel for your little one. The site is clearly separated into clothing and accessories for boys and girls from birth to 12 years. Pieces from the current range include the 'Pomme de Pin' (pine cone) hooded jacket and the 'La Vie En Rose', a soft pink dress with Peter Pan-style collar. A comprehensive nursery category includes the stunning 'Les Petits Lapins' collection featuring an adorable baby bunny on a mobile, bedding set, lamp shade and more!

GREAT FOR:
Clothing, toys, nursery décor

littletwig.com

USA

PURE & NATURAL BODY CARE

With the self-described philosophy of producing pure, natural bath and body products for babies and children, Little Twig is clear in its intention. Products are neatly categorised and include 'Bath Care', 'Bubble Fun', 'Body Care' and 'Accessories'. Products include 'Calm' shampoo and body wash, and 'Relax' baby oil. Not surprisingly the site's press section includes references to Gwyneth/Apple and Courtney/Coco as fans of this super stylish brand. Attractive gift sets are also available.

GREAT FOR:
Body care, accessories

millandmia.com   AUS

EXCLUSIVE CLOTHING & BEDDING

This incredibly chic site offers a range of high-end children's clothing, bedding and furniture. All products are locally made and combine simplicity with classic style. The unisex Basics range (0-3 months) is a highlight of the site and the bodysuits have served as the perfect baby gift on more than one occasion. The bedding range is also impressive and challenges the philosophy that baby manchester cannot be chic and contemporary. Orders can be placed by phone, fax or mail and an order form is provided online.

GREAT FOR: Clothing, nursery décor, furniture

modbaby.com.au   AUS

MERCHANDISE MADE FOR THE MODERN BABY

As its name says, this slick-looking site caters for the needs of the modern baby. Sharply designed and separated into clear categories including 'Bath', 'Sleepwear' and 'Indulge', Mod Baby is a no-nonsense destination for all things baby. Many items are imported exclusively from the USA, and the site also stocks a range of environmentally friendly, organic brands. Gift registry service available.

GREAT FOR: Furniture, bedding, décor, toys

modernnursery.com — USA

BEGIN LIFE IN STYLE

The mission of this site is clear – 'to make designing your little one's first surroundings simple and fun'. To this end, Modern Nursery includes everything a parent could want, from bedding to mobiles, and even play tents, to ensure your baby's life begins as you wish it to continue – in style. All products have a distinctly contemporary emphasis and the site is divided into clear categories including 'Furniture', 'Bedding', 'Toys' and 'Gifts'. The reversible polka dot blankets are a personal favourite and make a perfect unisex gift. The brightly coloured wall-stickers would be another welcome addition to any baby's space.

GREAT FOR:
Furniture, bedding, décor, toys

mvbabyandkids.com — USA

QUAINT FURNISHINGS & ACCESSORIES

This site – the online presence of California's Mill Valley Baby & Kids Company – stocks everything from furniture to linen to albums, strollers and toys. Whilst the initial listing may appear overwhelming, each category is quickly divided into sub-categories, making shopping simple. Highlights include the hand-embroidered Gordonsbury Company crib linen and mini-Adirondack rocking chairs. A selection of personalised gifts, including sweaters and mini-pillows, is also available.

GREAT FOR:
Nursery décor, bedding, clothing, toys

naturebaby.co.nz   NZ

NURTURING ORGANIC BABY PRODUCTS

For those who believe that 'organic' is code for hippy-inspired inferior merchandise, this site should challenge such assumptions. With a crisp, clear layout and superb products, Nature Baby is a one-stop shop for all your baby-related needs. From clothing to bedding and bathing ranges to food items and books, all items are natural and organic. Highlights include soft organic cotton sleepwear and bodysuits, together with organic merino wool blankets in a range of colours.

GREAT FOR:
Clothing, toys, bedding, bathing

neopolita.com   USA

PLUSH HAND-KNITS

This is a truly special site, offering what is described as 'soft serve' hats for babies. Hand-knitted with merino wool, there are currently 15 colours/flavours including banana split, chocolate chip and orange sherbet. But what would an ice-cream scoop be without a cone? Enter the newest item to the range – ponchos that look like waffle cones. And the quirky nature of this product doesn't stop there. All ice-cream hats are cleverly packaged in clear sundae containers, complete with a wooden ice-cream spoon. A range of hand-knitted blankets is also available.

GREAT FOR:
Clothing, blankets

nippazwithattitude.co.uk   UK

APPAREL FOR THE COOLEST BABIES & TODDLERS

Forget cutesy cartoon characters and smiling farm animals, today's babies want wit, humour and, most of all, some attitude. Browse this e-store for baby clothing with an edge, including body vests, T-shirts, sweat shirts, and bibs emblazoned with such gems as 'It's Gonna End in Tears' and 'Mama Ain't Raisin' no Fool'. Not for the faint-hearted or those who think only pink or blue is suitable for the under twos. But for the rest of us, a great site! A range of music for babies is also available, with classic tracks (think The Sex Pistols, Eminem and even Culture Club) recreated lullaby-style.

GREAT FOR:
Clothing, music

pamperedtot.com   USA

THE WORLD'S FINEST FOR YOUR MOST PRECIOUS

The brainchild of a former US advertising executive, this site is a chic take on the traditional baby boutique. The site includes clothing and accessories for babies and children up to six years, including a selection of practical yet fashionable 'Baby Basics'. 'On the Go' provides a fabulous selection of baby bags and changing mats while the 'Meal Time' collection features brightly coloured bibs, bowls and high chairs. Toys include crocheted animals by Anne-Claire Petit. If preferred, you can also shop by designer ranges, which include Burts Bees, Flora and Henri, and Zid Zid Kids.

GREAT FOR:
Clothing, décor, accessories, bedding

petitbateau.com
USA/FR

FRENCH FUN
This world famous French brand is synonymous with chic wardrobe essentials for the whole family. For babies in particular, this site features great basic apparel with a French feel. Whilst only a modest range is available for purchase online, highlights include a red long-sleeved tee with a contrasting marble grey stripe and a navy-and-white winter dress with ruffled wrist detail. Children's apparel is separated into 'Boy', 'Girl' and 'Newborns'. A range of classic T-shirts and bodysuits is also available.

GREAT FOR:
Clothing – babies, children, men and women

phibetababy.com
USA

HANDMADE GIFTS FOR BRILLIANT BABIES
Strange name, but great products. The site aims to offer shoppers hip baby and children's gifts combining modern fabrics with a whimsical design style. Most products are handmade and include hats, tees, blankets and (better than) booties. Designs include the 'Funky Chicken' tank and the 'Little Mac' bodysuit.

GREAT FOR:
Clothing, accessories, bedding, bags

pilo.ca

CAN

GREAT FOR:
Décor items

EXQUISITE HANDMADE HEIRLOOMS
This is one of my best online shopping finds. A discrete, soothing site featuring handmade cushions, bedding and linens made in Toronto, Canada. What Pi'lo lacks in quantity it more than makes up for in quality. The baby range is breathtaking and includes cotton and linen fabric alphabets and alphabet wall hangings in the softest linens. Personalised canvases and pocket pillows are also available.

rockyourbaby.com.au

AUS

GREAT FOR:
Clothing

ENFANT TERRIBLE COUTURE
The proprietors of this site recognise the importance of fashion as the sixth sense in the development of your treasured little loved one. Providing what they describe as 'fashion for the prematurely hip', Rock Your Baby features a collection of cotton T-shirts, bodysuits, hats, bibs and shoes for newborns up to three-year-olds. With more than 30 designs, including 'Future Feminist' and the cheeky 'Spit Happens', you're assured of a few laughs when you browse this site.

shescrafty.com NZ

VINTAGE-STYLE KNITWEAR

If, like me, you love the idea of hand-knitted infant wear and gifts, but do not have the time nor inclination to start knitting, you'll love Shescrafty. The site provides the stage for a range of adorable hand-knits made in New Zealand from organic merino wool. Whilst the collection is modest, the current range includes adorable booties and pixie-style hats, together with 'Fifi', a vintage-style toy canine. A custom knitting service is also available.

GREAT FOR:
Clothing, toys

speesees.com USA

ORGANIC COTTON BABY LINE

Of all the sights and sounds of Planet Earth, perhaps none are more fascinating to children of all ages than those from the animal world. Speesees is an organic cotton line featuring animals, from giraffes to seahorses, printed onto T-shirts, bodysuits and even yoga pants, for babies up to 24 months. Accessories including caps, bibs and booties complete the range. A plant-inspired collection is also available. The site also includes an informative profile of each of the animal species featured.

GREAT FOR:
Clothing, accessories

strawberrybaby.com   USA

GREAT FOR:
Toys, accessories, décor items

WHEN ONLY THE BEST WILL DO
Shopping for baby on this site is uncomplicated and fun. Products are separated into ranges including 'Bathtime, Bibs and Burps', 'Clothing' and 'Toys'. Bestsellers include the Poppy and Mimi keepsake books and the vintage astronaut hooded bath towel set. The site also features my favourite item – the Three Little Pigs hand-knitted finger puppets in a matching woollen drawstring pouch by Blabla.

urbanbaby.com.au   AUS

GREAT FOR:
Blankets, bathing, toys, clothing

INNOVATIVE BABY BUYS
At last, a funky yet practical site for the modern mum. From bottles to faux fur booties, Urban Baby blurs the line between essentials and extravagance. Easily divided into distinct categories, new items and monthly specials are also clearly displayed. A gift registry service is also available.

zacandzoe.com

USA

WHERE FUNCTION MEETS FUN

To some, having a baby means the end of matching furniture, replaced by 'baby friendly' merchandise that is practical but often very, very ugly. Zac and Zoé proves it doesn't have to be that way! Featuring an impressive collection of furniture and décor items, the site is easy to navigate, with clear product descriptions (including dimensions). The circular chalkboard table, in particular, would be a welcome addition to any family home, combining cutting-edge design whilst allowing your budding artiste to perfect their skills.

GREAT FOR:
Furniture, nursery décor, toys

a kid's world
FASHION, ACCESSORIES & FUN THINGS FOR THE UNDER-12s

abercrombiekids.com — USA

CLASSIC AMERICAN COLLECTIONS

Whilst this brand is perhaps better known for its preppy-style casual wear for adults, Abercrombie and Fitch also has an impressive children's line. Simply separated into 'Girls' and 'Boys', the collection includes super-soft tanks and sweaters with a classic American feel for girls, while boys will love the long-sleeved cotton polos and lightweight cargos. Fragrances and accessories, including belts and scarves, are also available.

GREAT FOR:
Clothing, accessories

---

allmineforkids.com.au — AUS

PRACTICAL PERSONALISED PRODUCTS

It's a fact that, for children of all ages, there's nothing quite as special as a personalised gift. The kids in your life will love the quality range by All Mine For Kids, which includes blankets, beanbags, cushions and towels. Featured blanket designs include a dinosaur, star, or a flower, and all items are personalised with your child's name or initials. Other highlights include beanbags made from high-quality anti-pill polar fleece. All products are Australian made.

GREAT FOR:
Bedding, décor items

bestnco.com

USA

ELEGANT SPECIAL-OCCASION WEAR

Think traditional hand-knitted cardigans, classic navy blazers and smocked party dresses, and you have Best & Co. Started by Suzie Hilfiger (wife of famous fashion identity Tommy), this site offers a luxurious selection of clothing for infants, boys and girls. The collection is particularly appropriate for special-occasion dressing. A range of beautiful shoes, blankets and toys is also available.

GREAT FOR:
Clothing, accessories

bluepaw.com.au

AUS

CREATIVE ART FOR YOUNG MINDS

It's time to ditch the tired posters blue-tacked to the wall. Boasting 'artwork to inspire imagination in young minds', Blue Paw features a range of artwork suitable for children of all ages. Designs are separated into distinct categories including 'Animals', 'Girls', 'Boys' and 'ABC'. Favourites include bright fire engines, sailboats against a gingham background and a jolly juggling lion. Each artwork is personally signed by the artist, and personalised designs are available. It's an affordable way to add an artistic edge to any child's room.

GREAT FOR:
Décor items

boden.co.uk   UK

BRITISH WARDROBE ESSENTIALS
Launched in 1996, the children's range from Boden is a web highlight. Look out for pom pom ponchos and velvet trim sweaters for girls, and duck down jackets for the boys. The site also has a great selection of sleepwear, including cotton pj sets and snugly dressing-gowns. A range of shoes and accessories including belts and hats is also available. An excellent FAQ section will answer all your shopping queries.

GREAT FOR:
Clothing, accessories

butterflykiss.com.au   AUS

ADORABLE PJS FOR COOL KIDS
This label produces adorable pyjamas for the fashion-savvy children in your life. All pjs are 100% cotton and are available for children from newborn to six years. The 'Surfer Boy' set with a short-sleeved top and short pants with a palm tree print, and the 'My Mum Loves Me' design are favourites. Pjs are made for a snug fit and with extra long tops to ensure little tummies stay toasty all night long.

GREAT FOR:
Sleepwear

chalk.com.au

AUS

EDUCATIONAL TOYS

Chances are your children don't believe that 'toys' and 'educational' are concepts that belong together. The good news is that Chalk may change that view. Stocking hundreds of toys from around the world, this site specialises in educational games and products. Current brands include Living & Learning, Playmobil and Tree of Knowledge. Searching through categories including 'On the Move', 'Sporty' and 'Pretend', you'll find a comprehensive selection of merchandise to stimulate the minds of children of all ages, whilst still providing hours of good old-fashioned fun.

GREAT FOR:
Toys, games

childrensplace.com

USA

SPECIALTY RETAILER OF CHILDREN'S WARE

For high-quality apparel at reasonable prices, you can't go past Children's Place. Catering for children from newborn to 10 years, the site clearly displays its wares for 'Newborns', 'Baby Girls', 'Big Girls', 'Baby Boys', 'Big Boys' and 'Toys'. The boy's range – particularly jeans and pants – is consistently good. A great destination for your ever-growing offspring.

GREAT FOR:
Clothing, toys, accessories

cocoacrayon.com
USA

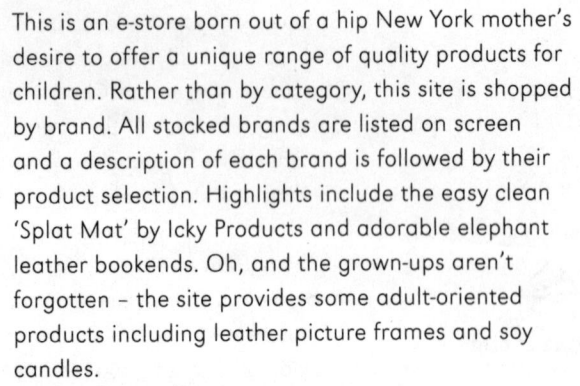

TOP OF THE TOTS
This is an e-store born out of a hip New York mother's desire to offer a unique range of quality products for children. Rather than by category, this site is shopped by brand. All stocked brands are listed on screen and a description of each brand is followed by their product selection. Highlights include the easy clean 'Splat Mat' by Icky Products and adorable elephant leather bookends. Oh, and the grown-ups aren't forgotten – the site provides some adult-oriented products including leather picture frames and soy candles.

GREAT FOR:
Clothing, toys, accessories

coolgiftsforkids.co.uk
UK

KIDS' GIFTS THAT MAKE A STATEMENT
No surprises here! This site actually provides really cool gifts for kids up to about seven years of age. Gifts are easily separated into age categories from newborn to 12 months to five to seven years. There is also a 'Baby' section and a range of christening-specific gifts. For the musically inclined two-year-old in your life consider the colourful wooden instruments, whilst for seven-year-old girls you can't go past the 'Beauty Spa Party Kit'.

GREAT FOR:
Toys, décor, clothing

craftsburykids.com
USA

DISTINCTIVE HANDCRAFTED COLLECTIONS
You won't find the latest action figure or playstation game on this site. Rather, Craftsbury Kids has attempted to capture the magic of childhood through a selection of traditional toys and products for the young and young at heart. Each piece is lovingly handcrafted by a team of artisans and product highlights include the Lion Pop-Out Toy and a Gingerbread Floor Quilt.

GREAT FOR:
Toys, décor, clothing

estkids.com.au
AUS

BEAUTIFUL BEDDING, CLOTHING & GIFTS
This Melbourne-based store offers an impossibly cute range of children's décor items, clothing and toys. The Estkids look is described as 'chic with a classic twist' and has a strong emphasis on French gingham and colourful prints. The 'Sailor Sam' cotton quilt cover in red with navy stripes and feature patches is sure to be a hit with any little boy. Also look out for the best-selling mini-couch with a quilted polycotton cover suitable for children up to seven years. A baby range including crib and cot bedding is also available.

GREAT FOR:
Décor items

floraandhenri.com — USA

CHILDREN'S CLOTHING

Established in 1998, the Flora and Henri range features vintage-inspired fashion for children up to 12 years. Many pieces are produced in soft, natural colours including shades of grey and caramel. The current collection includes a linen party dress with a soft jersey collar and a boy's wool tweed coat with wooden buttons. The 'Essentials Range' includes a high-quality selection of cotton tees, briefs and leggings.

GREAT FOR:
Clothing

gltc.co.uk — UK

CREATIVE GIFTS FOR ALL OCCASIONS

A fab selection of toys, bedding and imaginative gifts awaits you at gltc – Great Little Trading Company. Click onto 'Creative Fun' and take a look at the 'Make Your Own Twinkly Tiara Kit', and then move to 'Toys & Games' for an unbeatable range of pretend play pieces. The site also has a great range of personalised pencils, books, puzzles and ceramic plates.

GREAT FOR:
Toys, décor, furniture

growgrowgrow.com
USA

COMFY COTTON CLOTHING
At Grow, Grow, Grow you'll find a collection of clever and comfortable cotton play-wear for children of all ages. Founded in 1998, the site offers more than 20 clothing items, including T-shirts, dresses and pullovers, featuring original handdrawn illustrations. In 'Endearing Terms' you'll find the 'I'm Crabby' design and in 'Good Enough to Eat' you can't go past the 'Cupcake'. In addition to clothing, bedding, wall art and place-mats, together with a range of adult-sized apparel, are also available.

GREAT FOR:
Clothing

hamleys.co.uk
UK

THE BEST OF BRITISH TOYS
Relive your childhood browsing through this e-store from iconic British toy retailer Hamleys. With arts and craft supplies, dress-ups, construction sets, action figures and the traditional teddy, if there's a toy made, chances are you'll find it here. Shop by product, brand, age or price range, or enter the name of the exact toy you're after. The site also features a range of signature Hamleys toys including traditional train sets, double decker buses and black cabs, all emblazoned with the Hamleys label. This year's best-sellers include 'Amazing Amanda', a realistic interactive doll, and 'Street Gliders', two-wheeler skates that easily convert to walkers.

GREAT FOR:
Toys, games

imadethat.com

USA

FURNITURE KIDS CAN MAKE

The DIY revolution has hit the playground, thanks largely to sites like this. Imadethat enables kids aged four to eight years to launch into a range of mini-building projects including the 'Take Along' toolbox, the 'Sir Steps a Lot' stool and the 'Mister Feet' table. Fortunately no nails are used, with all pieces neatly fitting together and secured with wooden pegs and glue. Depending on a child's age, most products take about an hour and a half to complete, and paint can also be purchased to provide a personal touch. Click on to 'Proud Kids' to see some talented youngsters showing off their finished work.

GREAT FOR:
Toys, activities

jigsaw.net

AUS

TOYS TO EDUCATE YOUNG MINDS

Jigsaw believes that toys, far from being unimportant, are the means through which children grow, learn and develop. For over 30 years, Jigsaw has been a recognised leader in the field of educational-focused toys and games. Whilst traditionally available through direct selling, the online store on this site offers an excellent selection of products including jigsaws, games, books and wooden puzzles. The site also offers some important advice on toy safety and related issues. The company recently announced a joint partnership with Highlights-Jigsaw in the USA.

GREAT FOR:
Toys, games

kids-chairs.co.uk   UK

MADE-TO-ORDER CHILDREN'S FURNITURE

The name says it all, really – this site sells chairs for kids. It also sells a range of beds and décor accessories with a distinctly stylish edge. Styles include the 'Mamma Mia' designs available in a range of fabrics and suitable for children aged two to nine years. The 'Kids' Sleepover Bed' is another highlight, providing a nifty alternative to the traditional folding bed, converting from a contemporary chair to a bed in seconds.

GREAT FOR:
Furniture

kidsown.net.nz   NZ

HAIR-CARE MADE ESPECIALLY FOR CHILDREN

Today's kids seem to have their own phones, lap tops and credit cards. So it's not surprising that they also have their own hair-care products. This site offers a range of shampoos, conditioners and styling products formulated specifically for the sensitive scalps of babies and children. You'll find a super gentle baby shampoo, a daily low-lathering shampoo, and the remarkable 'After Swim' shampoo which removes salt and chlorine from children's hair. A great new addition is 'Ponytail Rescue' – ideal for styling plaits, pigtails and ballet buns.

GREAT FOR:
Hair-care products

kule.com
USA

UNIQUELY MODERN CLASSICS

Founder and designer Nikki Kule describes the Kule range as offering uniquely modern versions of fashion classics. Think striped knits and corduroy pants for boys, and a cashmere v-neck sweater with an attached floral cotton collar for girls. The line is completed by a range of suitably fashionable junior footwear. Coordinated accessories including detailed hats and scarves are also featured.

GREAT FOR:
Clothing, accessories

letterbox.co.uk
UK

BRIGHT IDEAS FOR KIDS

Packed with a great collection of toys, games, outdoor play items and décor accessories, Letterbox provides an unparalleled range of toys for babies, toddlers and children. From traditional favourites including Russian Nesting Dolls, through to the popular Cosmic Flashing Scooter, this site has it all. The 'Find a Gift' section is a great feature, allowing you to make age/budget-appropriate gift selections with ease. The site also has a great range of personalised gifts including plates, bags and calendars. Many designs are exclusive to Letterbox.

GREAT FOR:
Toys, games

lillylolly.com.au   AUS

QUALITY CHILDREN'S MANCHESTER

One of the web's best kept secrets, Lilly & Lolly is packed with quality children's manchester and bedding accessories. You'll love the 'Nautical Stripe' range featuring a smart red, white and blue striped cotton doona cover, with matching pillowcase and monogrammed cushion, complemented by coordinating pjs. The 'Little Stars' collection is a terrific unisex range available in blue, red, pink and lime. A selection of furniture items is also available, including coloured 'Life Saver' stools and an upholstered bed available in your choice of fabrics.

GREAT FOR:
Bedding, décor items

littlehouse.com.au   AUS

BEAUTIFULLY CRAFTED CHILDREN'S BED LINEN

The label of choice for style-savvy parents and design-aware kids, Little House boasts a stunning collection of coordinated cot sheets, blankets, doona covers, quilts and cushions. The site is neatly separated into shopping categories including 'Cot Linen', 'Blankets' and 'Quilts'. In recent years the range has expanded to include items such as dressing-gowns, bibs, lampshades and aprons. Designs, named after the owner's children and their friends, feature creative motifs including butterflies, bees, stars, trains and country & western stripes. All products are Australian-made.

GREAT FOR:
Bedding, décor items

minidecor.com.au

AUS

SMALL-SCALE STYLE

When only the best in international children's clothing, toys and décor accessories will do, log on to Mini Décor. Selling a carefully selected range of sophisticated products, this site stocks more than 30 brands including Anne-Claire Petit, Trumpette and Elephantito. Take a peek at the mini-embroidered suitcases by Room Seven and the contemporary elephant-themed mobile from Denmark's Filensted. All purchases are sent in stylish gift bags.

GREAT FOR:
Toys, décor items, clothing

miotowels.com.au

AUS

MONOGRAMMED TOWELS & ACCESSORIES

There was a time when towels were boring, but not anymore thanks to sites like this. The team at Mio Towels produces a range of kids' towels and accessories all personally monogrammed with your child's name. Designs include a zippy red fire engine, a pink fairy, a row of cowboys, and a red, white and blue sailboat, all embroidered on quality white towels. The product range also includes monogrammed library bags and aprons.

GREAT FOR:
Towels

modernseed.com   USA

FURNITURE, FASHION & DESIGN FOR KIDS

Modern Seed specialises in contemporary furnishing and fashion for kids. Founder Melissa Pfieffer wanted to create the definitive destination for 'all things modern for the mini'. The collection includes lighting, bedding, clothing and toys. Hot picks include 'Fat Boy Island', a novel alternative to the beanbag, and the range of Alexander Girard signature tees. Many items are exclusive to Modern Seed and are clearly identified on the site.

GREAT FOR:
Furniture, décor items

oliebollen.com   USA

COOL THINGS FOR KIDS

Question: What is an oliebollen? Answer: a Dutch deep-fried donut. Not exactly a clear choice for the name of a children's e-store, but typical of the unusual and slightly off-centre humour that characterises this site. Oliebollen.com features toys, clothing, books and décor items. Click on to 'Adorable Clothes' for a peek at the Andy Warhol hoodie and the Ribbon Stripe dress set. Current hip toys include the American retro Pedal Estate Wagon and the Kids' Yoga Deck.

GREAT FOR:
Clothing, décor items, toys, games

piscessoap.com
USA

SOAPS ALMOST GOOD ENOUGH TO EAT

'Come on kids, get out of those clothes, into the bath, and don't forget your cheeseburgers.' Not words one would expect to hear from an in-control parent but, thanks to this site, a not-so-warped remark. You see, Pisces Soap makes a range of innovative kids' soaps shaped as food items including a grilled cheese sandwich, chocolate brownies, bagels, burgers and cupcakes. All soaps are made from hypoallergenic ingredients and are infused with vanilla, lemon and chocolate scents. For bigger kids, a collection of life-like garden soaps is also available.

GREAT FOR:
Soaps

pokkadots.com
USA

PRODUCTS TO MAKE LITTLE PEOPLE HAPPY

Pokkadots aims to make little people happy and it does so with a site filled with clothing, toys, décor items and books sure to be a hit with any discerning youngster. Featured brands include Zapato clothing, Dwell bedding, and knitted toys by Blabla. In the 'Imaginative Play' section you can move from an operational mini-work bench to a dream kitchen with a mere mouse click. Take a look at the 'Sale' section for some great designer discounts. Great gifts for parents, grandparents and siblings are also available. The site was awarded the *Forbes* magazine 'Best of the Web' award for Baby Gear (2004).

GREAT FOR:
Clothing, décor items, books, toys

raspberryripple.com.au

AUS

GREAT FOR:
Blankets, towels, placemats

PERSONALISED CHILDREN'S GIFTS

What's in a name? A lot, according to Raspberry Ripple. Producing a range of blankets, pjs, towels and bags, all personalised with your child's name or initials, this is one of my favourite e-stores. The Swimming Bag is made from bright cotton gingham with a waterproof lining, while the mini-aprons are plastic covered and emblazoned with the name of your junior Jamie Oliver. Personalised photo albums, artwork and sheets are also available. All products are 100% Australian-made.

seedchild.com.au

AUS

GREAT FOR:
Clothing

CLOTHES FOR LIFE'S LITTLE ADVENTURES

With the mantra that 'the future belongs to things that grow', Seed features a range of comfortable yet stylish clothing and accessories for kids from birth to eight years. For boys, it's nautical-inspired striped tees and racy cargo pants, while for girls it's all about layered dresses and embroidered tees. The site also includes a 'How to Wear' section providing some mix-and-match outfit ideas. A range of traditional-style toys, including junior quoits and wooden trains, is also available.

sonsanddaughtersinc.com — USA

IMPECCABLE IMPORTED CLOTHING & ACCESSORIES

A gold star for good design and an impressive product menu goes to this site. From organic cotton clothing, shoes, books and room accessories, Sons and Daughters covers the spectrum of traditional to contemporary kids' merchandise with ease. Product highlights include the Fleurville Lunch Pack and the moon rocket fantasy playhouse.

GREAT FOR:
Clothing, toys

theredballoon.com — USA

A UNIQUE STORE FOR KIDS

This e-store stocks only the best in fashion, books, toys and décor accessories for kids. The site is neatly designed with products categorised by purpose such as 'For Reading', 'For Wearing' and 'For Decorating'. Featured clothing lines are suitable for children up to six years and currently include colour-blocked angora sweaters from Peru and a tailored paisley single-breasted coat. Junior room accessories include Lucy and Michael play tents and designer night-lights from Whimsy Design. Many items can also be personalised.

GREAT FOR:
Clothing, toys, books, décor items

thinkbutton.com

USA

GREAT PRODUCTS FOR GROWING MINDS

Environmental awareness. Creative expression. Social understanding. Not usually phrases associated with children's products, but key concepts in the selection of award-winning toys, games and books at Thinkbutton. This site provides what it describes as 'knowledge products for the growing mind' and is clearly separated into distinct categories including 'Product Type' (including Science and Nature Kits) and age groups (from newborn to 12 years plus). Embark on a counting adventure through Tanzania or start building with the inflatable building block set – the options are endless.

GREAT FOR:
Educational toys & games

toottoottoys.com.au

AUS

TRAIN-THEMED TOY WORLD

Whilst, as a wise musician once said, times are a changing, when it comes to toys some things stay the same – little boys (and girls) love their trains. The team at Toot Toot Toys are well aware of this enduring trend and boast one of the premier online e-stores for toy train and train-related merchandise. The site includes an incredible range of competitively priced Thomas the Tank Engine products, clearly separated into categories such as 'Wooden Railway', 'Books & Learning' and 'Party Supplies'. Fisher Price Geo Trax train items, together with a selection of train toys, games and puzzles, are also featured.

GREAT FOR:
Toys

toy-choice.co.uk
UK

WOODEN & TRADITIONAL CHILDREN'S TOYS

There was a time when the term mobile was only used when discussing nursery décor, when a mouse was merely a small hairy rodent, and children's toys were made only of wood. This site takes you back to that time with an exquisite selection of quality wooden toys, farms, doll houses, fire stations and more. Whilst the site may not have the bells and whistles of other sites in this category, the product speaks for itself. The Giant Noah's Ark contains 10 pairs of handpainted animals and the Ark has a lift-off deck, while the Dollhouse collection includes not just the house, but also a choice of furniture and outdoor accessories.

GREAT FOR:
Toys, games

urchin.co.uk
UK

COLOURFUL LIVING FOR KIDS

Kids love colour and Urchin knows it. This site is positively bursting with bold and bright toys, games and accessories for children. Choose from selections including 'Kids Parties', 'Kids Room' and 'Kids Travel' for an impressive collection of products. Best-sellers include 'Candeloo', an innovative night-light, the personalised wooden name train, and the colour change bath ducks. A great selection of practical items for parents including car seats, strollers and family travel accessories are also featured.

GREAT FOR:
Toys, games, décor items

the beauty zone
LOTIONS, POTIONS, MAKE-UP & FRAGRANCES

aedes.com
USA

INDULGE YOUR SENSES
Beauty junkies have long been in awe of the old world European charm of New York's Aedes de Venustas boutique. Their online store features an impressive range of fragrances, body products and skin-care collections, many of which are not readily available in Australia. These include Acqua Di Biella perfume (apparently a celebrity favourite) and the mysterious Costes, the signature scent of the exclusive Hotel Costes in Paris. Côté Bastide sits side by side the sophisticated collection by Italy's Etro and pomegranate soap by Santa Maria Novella.

GREAT FOR:
Fragrances, bathing products

apothia.com
USA

BEAUTY WITH STYLE
As the online offshoot of the renowned Apothia at Fred Segal, this site features heaps of colour, movement and, most of all, product! Merchandise is clearly categorised and a 'hot box' collection of what Apothia considers the best brands is also included. Aside from the traditional beauty staples from Keihl's, many of the brands will be not so familiar, including handcrafted soaps by Mistral, Provence and the New York-themed range of perfumes such as New York Fling and Park Avenue by Bond #9.

GREAT FOR:
Fragrances, bath & body, make-up

bathandunwind.co.uk
UK

GREAT FOR:
Bath & shower treats, candles

LUXURY BATHING COLLECTION
Not surprisingly, this e-store is all about relaxing and de-stressing at the end of a busy day. With a range of high-quality bath and spa products, over two dozen international brands are featured. Click on to 'Bath and Shower' for Di Palomo's indulgent bath truffles or 'Candles' for the Orange Blossom candle by Creation Mathias. Continuing the relaxation theme, a range of waffle bathrobes, sea sponges and spa pillows is also available. The 'Gift' range includes beautifully packaged gift sets for any occasion.

beautyhabit.com
USA

GREAT FOR:
Bath & body, make-up, fragrances

ADDICTIVE PERSONAL CARE PRODUCTS
Beauty Habit promises the finest personal care products from all over the world. From aromatherapy, to candles, make-up and perfumes, the site should satisfy the needs of the beauty aware everywhere. More than 150 premium brands are featured and you can shop by your favourite label or product type. Take a look at the Italian i Profumi Di Firenze range of hand-blended perfumes and Austria's Nanadebary fragrances.

b-glowing.com — USA

THE BEST IN BOUTIQUE BEAUTY

A self-confessed beauty addict started this site and, from the incredible range of products available, her addiction shows no sign of abating. The store has a focus on independent brands, together with some hard-to-find imported ranges. For cleansing, exfoliating, toning, moisturising and tanning, the skincare range is unmatched, and the bath/body range looks after your bod from your pearly whites to tired tootsies. The fragrance collection from the Moroccan-inspired Aqaba is a stand-out. The story behind each label provides some interesting background to your chosen brand.

GREAT FOR: Body-care, make-up, perfume

bidwellbotanicals.com — USA

LUXURIOUSLY NATURAL SKINCARE

Combining organically grown herbs and botanicals with local ingredients, Bidwell Botanicals produces a range of bath and body-care treats. Specific product categories include handmade soaps, spa/bath products, facial care items, and scents for the male persuasion. The spa range is fab – new items include the Spiced Pumpkin Scrub and, for those with more than just a sweet tooth, look out for the Hot Chocolate Body Scrub. A great 'Gift' section is also featured, with presents able to be forwarded directly to the recipient.

GREAT FOR: Handmade soap, facial care, bathing products

blissworld.com

USA

ONLINE BEAUTY FROM NEW YORK'S HOTTEST SPA

A mecca for spa lovers everywhere, this site allows you to enter the sacred and soothing world of one of New York and London's hottest spas. You'll find all the products used for the famous spa treatments, together with a range of accessories including angora bed socks and cashmere robes. In terms of beauty and body care, we're talking cleansers, toners, exfoliators, masks and treatment products, together with eye formulas, body-care lotions and make-up. The anti-ageing products are particularly impressive and include the new Bliss Sleeping Peel kit containing a mask, serum, gel and cleansing cream.

GREAT FOR:
Skincare, body-care, anti ageing products

burtsbees.com

USA

BEAUTY FROM BEESWAX

Even if you're not into the beauty thing, you'll love Burt's Bees. With a range of practical personal care products, the collection includes beeswax lip balm, lip gloss, cleansers, toners, moisturisers and natural remedies. Check out the 'Gift & Kits' section for a hand-picked selection of best-selling products in re-usable bags. Starter kits for the skin-care range are also available. For great savings, don't forget 'Burt's Outlet' for some discontinued, overstocked, or slightly less than perfectly packaged items at 25–50% off.

GREAT FOR:
Lip balms, facial care, hair-care

cakebeauty.com

CAN

BODY-CARE GOOD ENOUGH TO EAT

Lauded as Canada's hottest bath and beauty line, Cake Beauty features an indulgent line of delectable cremes, scrubs and suds, including 'Dessert's on Me', a whipped body spread with Swiss white chocolate and wild cherry flavours. New additions to the collection include the Satin Sugar refreshing hair and body mist, and the Deserted Island moisturising body glaze. A range of six gift sets, presented in signature boxes with fuchsia satin lining, is also available.

GREAT FOR:
Body cremes, body-care, gifts

cobigelow.com

USA

APOTHECARY FROM THE BIG APPLE

Tucked amid the hustle and bustle of New York's West Village is this acclaimed 167-year-old apothecary store. With homeopathic remedies, hair-care, personal care collections and signature perfume oils, their e-store features only the best of the best. Product lines are separated into 'Personal Care', 'Apothecary', 'Baby Care', 'Home Fragrance' and 'Gifts', while featured brands include Cobigelow's own line, together with leading international names like Aqua di Palma and Sundari. A printable product catalogue can be downloaded from the site.

GREAT FOR:
Personal care, homeopathic products, home fragrances

cowshedproducts.co.uk

UK

CULT HANDMADE HAIR & BODY PRODUCTS

Perhaps not the place one would first expect to find high-end beauty and body products, Cowshed features a selection of skincare, hair-care as well as spa products and body oils. Boasting rich texture and luscious aromas, the brand is a UK best-seller. And, just when you thought the beauty industry had no sense of humour comes the 'Grubby Cow Cleansing Milk', the 'Cowlick Hairwash', and the 'Raging Bull Invigorating Massage Oil'. No products are tested on animals and, in case you're wondering, the name Cowshed derives from the original use of the building now used as the day spa in the UK.

GREAT FOR:
Skincare, essential oils, spa collection

ebubbles.com

USA

SPECIALTY BATH & BEAUTY PRODUCTS

This site is a one-stop shop for pampering products for the bath and body. Shoppers can choose to make their selection based on a category, such as 'By User' or 'By Fragrance', or go straight to their favourite brands. One of the more unusual ranges is Bath Ice Cream, which promises to transform your tub into a tantalising treatment bath with a single scoop. Other featured brands include the Inis sea range, the Cucina kitchen hand-care collection, and Nesti Dante soaps from Florence. A range of gift ideas is also provided.

GREAT FOR:
Bath & body oils, body lotions, massage products

evolu.com.au
NZ

RADIANT SKINCARE
Founded on the philosophy that great skincare is more than how you look, this site wants you to feel good in your skin. To that end, Evolu sells a botanical skin-care collection incorporating facial products, body-care items and a travel range. One of the newest additions is the Quenching Hydramask, a rich and hydrating mask for thirsty complexions. All skincare types are catered for in the range and, if you're not sure of your type, click onto the 'Skindividualiser' to help find the best products for your individual needs.

GREAT FOR:
Skincare

eyeslipsface.com
USA

SIMPLE, LUXURIOUS BEAUTY TOOLS
The name says it all really – this site (also known as e.l.f.) showcases beauty and make-up products at value-for-money prices. Shoppers are encouraged to build their own make-up bag, choosing from great mascaras, eye liners, lip gloss, concealers, blushers and powders. Nails are not forgotten – a super selection of nail lacquers and accessories is also featured. Finish off in 'Brushes & Tools' for a range of competitively priced products. For those not sure of their best look, the 'Achieve the Look' section gives you step-by-step instructions for more than 10 make-up looks.

GREAT FOR:
Make-up, make-up tools

florisoflondon.com
UK

OLD-SCHOOL LUXURY FRAGRANCES
By appointment to HRH Her Majesty the Queen no less, Floris of London is an old-school perfumery. Founded in 1730, the brand is synonymous with timeless perfumes in traditionally elegant packaging. You won't find any off-the-wall fragrances here, instead admire the classics, which include Tuberose, Vetiver and Sandalwood. Luxury soap, shaving, bathing and home fragrance products complete the collection. The 'Fragrance List' section provides detailed information on individual fragrances, allowing for carefully considered online perfume selections.

GREAT FOR:
Fragrances – men, women, home

fragrancenet.com
USA

BRAND-NAME FRAGRANCES AT UNBEATABLE PRICES
Boasting more than 8000 brand-name fragrances, skin-care and hair-care products, this e-store, established in 1997, sells a lot more than just perfume. It also guarantees the authenticity of all its stock, which is priced at up to 70% off recommended retail prices. Allow yourself plenty of time to explore the site, preferably brand by brand, to ensure you don't miss any new or unexpected items. A selection of mini-fragrances is also available, which allows you to try a few new scents before making a full bottle commitment.

GREAT FOR:
Fragrances – men & women

fragrancex.com
USA

DISCOUNTED FRAGRANCES & SKINCARE
Once upon a time there was a girl (me) whose favourite perfume (Nocturnes De Caron) went missing. She searched high and low in every store, for weeks on end, but to no avail. Eventually she found this site, was reunited with three gleaming bottles of her signature scent and lived happily ever after. The moral of this fairytale is, if there's any perfume you are having difficulty tracking down, try FragranceX for over 9500 brands at great prices. The site also stocks skincare and make-up ranges.

GREAT FOR:
Fragrances - men & women, skincare, make-up

giannarose.com
USA

EXQUISITE PERSONAL CARE
A recognised leader in the design and manufacturing of a selection of exquisite soaps and personal care products, Gianna Rose oozes romance and class. Shop by 'Product' or 'Collection' for lavish bar soaps, lotions, creams, draw liners and candles. Current collections include 'From the Garden', 'Savon Delicate' and 'Verre d'Ocean'. The triple-milled vegetable soaps are especially decadent, promising to add a new dimension to bath or shower time.

GREAT FOR:
French milled soaps

gloss.com

USA

THE ULTIMATE BEAUTY DESTINATION

A unique partnership between beauty leaders Chanel, Clarins and Estée Lauder, Gloss is a utopia of beauty products. The site features more than 5000 items from the best in beauty, which include, in addition to the majors, Bobbi Brown, Jo Malone, La Mer and Stila. Browse through collections including 'Make-up', 'Skin-care', and 'Fragrance' by either brand or product category. Look out for super deals detailed in the 'Special Offers' section. A impressive men's range is also featured.

GREAT FOR:
Make-up, skincare, fragrances

goldendoorskincare.com

USA

CALIFORNIA'S HOTTEST SPA CHECKS INTO CYBERSPACE

Sure you may prefer to experience these products in the luxurious spa and fitness retreat of the same name, but for a touch of this world-renowned health and beauty phenomenon in the comfort of your own home, try this site. The products featured are the same as those used at the spa and include facial care, bath/body-care, sun protection and men's skincare. 'Bath and Body' is particularly impressive and includes the best-selling 'Signature Collection Citrus Blend Shower Gel'. Any traveller should invest in a pack of 'Soothing Eye Pads' – the perfect pick-me-up for tired peepers, particularly after flying.

GREAT FOR:
Skincare, bath & body-care

histoiresdeparfums.com FR

PRESTIGIOUS FRENCH PERFUMERY

Creating unique fragrances made according to the finest traditional French methods, this e-store is a window into a world of luxury and prestige. Certainly not for the discount shopper, fragrances are categorised into 'Eau de Parfums', 'Eau de Cologne', 'Bath & Body' and 'Home' lines. Described as 'memories etched in scent', rather than names, the parfums have been given numbers representing the year of birth of a significant historical figure. The 'Home' line promises the finishing touch to your abode and includes porcelain candle holders, garden incense and ambiance spray.

GREAT FOR:
Personal fragrances, home fragrances

jomalone.com UK

COUTURE SKINCARE

A favourite amongst chic Londoners and Park Avenue Princesses, Jo Malone offers what it terms 'couture skincare' complemented by a collection of luxurious bath, body and home fragrance products. Perfumes (or colognes as they are referred to on this site) are divided into 'Spicy', 'Woody', 'Citrus', 'Fruity' and 'Floral' scents, with original and sometimes unexpected aroma combinations. The skin-care range described as 'revolutionary' by many beauty writers, incorporates a range of products used either as stand-alone treatments or part of a more comprehensive skincare regime.

GREAT FOR:
Skincare, bath & body-care

kiehls.com

USA

OLD-STYLE SKIN- & BODY-CARE

Looking for no-nonsense, results-driven skin-, hair- and body-care products? Then head straight to Kiehl's. Established in New York more than 150 years ago, the range represents the blending of cosmetic, pharmaceutical, herbal and medicinal research. Using the finest ingredients, the range has items suitable for the whole family. For cleansers, scrubs, toners, serums, body lotions, fragrance, skincare and hair treatments, few products come close to Kiehl's. Oh, and forget extravagant packaging. All Kiehl's products are simply labelled in recyclable plastic containers. No products are tested on animals.

GREAT FOR:
Skincare, hair-care, body-care

lipmedic.com

USA

INTERNATIONAL LIP BALM BOUTIQUE

Lipmedic is described as 'nirvana for your lips'. With over 500 lip balms in more than 100 fabulous flavours, the site brings together possibly the largest ever selection of unique lip products. Selection criteria include 'Organic & Vegan Balms', 'Exotic & Foreign Balms' and 'Fun & Different Balms'. You can also make your selection by flavour, and these include apple pie, bubblegum, champagne, strawberry sundae and vanilla butterscotch. Featured brands include Beeswork, Brush on a Smile, Ecolips and Smack.

GREAT FOR:
Lip balms & salves

littleshopofbeauty.com

USA

CUSTOM-MADE BATH & BEAUTY LUXURIES

Little Shop of Beauty promises the ultimate in bath and body luxury. Product lines include body creams, bath oils, perfumes, cosmetics and room fragrances, all available in more than 600 scents. But we're not talking merely French vanilla or a citrus blend, at this e-store its more banana nut bread, biscotti, cherry cola, coconut milk or beach baby aromas. If you choose, you can even try scent blending for a truly personalised product. Who says sweet and savoury can't mix!

GREAT FOR:
Bathing products, fragrances, body-care

lusciouscargo.com

USA

LUXURY FRAGRANCES & GIFTS

For elegant and highly coveted perfumes, bath/body products and home fragrances, look no further than Luscious Cargo. The site is clearly laid out and has a very informative FAQ section, which should cover any shopper queries. Some of the brands stocked will be familiar whilst many, such as Dinner by Bobo, Patyka, and Vie Luxe may not. From the traditional French style of Diptyque to the contemporary metro chic of perfumes by Bond No. 9, New York, this site ensures that all scentual preferences are catered for. Click on 'New Cargo' for new stock arrivals.

GREAT FOR:
Fragrances, bath & body-care

meccacosmetica.com.au   AUS

INTERNATIONAL 'MUST HAVES' FOR FACE & BODY

Looking good is no easy task, but fortunately e-stores like this make the job a little simpler. Boasting make-up, skincare, fragrance and bathing products, Mecca Cosmetica stocks a collection of cutting-edge international merchandise. Click on to 'Mecca's Must Haves' for the newest and hottest beauty essentials, which currently include 'Kai Body Glow' and 'Nars Make-up Primer'. A range of signature Mecca Cosmetica branded products includes a 'Velvet Glove Hand Hydrator' and the 'Barefoot Beauty Foot Scrub'.

GREAT FOR:
Make-up, skincare, fragrances

moltonbrown.co.uk   UK

MODERN BRITISH BEAUTY

Now well into its 31st year, Molton Brown is an iconic British manufacturer of luxury beauty and lifestyle products. The range includes skincare, body therapy items, make-up and a travel collection. New products include a 'Warming Eucalyptus and Ginger Body Scrub' and the 'Active Defence City Day Hydrator'. A handcrafted range of luggage is available, including the stylish leather 'Molton Brown Stowaway' and the 'Molton Brown City Flyer' wash bag.

GREAT FOR:
Body-care, skincare

philosophy.com

USA

WHERE THE BEST COSMETIC IS GREAT-LOOKING SKIN

If you like your skincare with a good boost of humour, then Philosophy is for you. Forget the gleaming smiles of size 4 supermodels, this site is big on babies – a way Philosophy believes highlights the simple pleasures of life. The site features products for women, men and children, including skin-care, bath, make-up and fragrance ranges. Products include the cleverly named 'Hope in a Jar' for the face, the 'Big Skinny' body-firming serum and 'Soul Owner' for the feet. Shoppers can also select items by recipient (such as for her, for a neighbour, or for a soul-mate) or occasion (including thankyou, house-warming, and get well).

GREAT FOR:
Skincare, bath & body-care, make-up

planetbeauty.com

USA

ONE-STOP BEAUTY SHOP

Planet is an understatement – this site provides more like a universe of beauty and related merchandise. More than 100 international brands are featured and clearly separated into categories including 'Skincare', 'Nails', 'Make-up', and 'Tools'. Don't miss the revolutionary 'Fake Bake' self tanner, 'Lip Explosion' instant lip plumper, and 'Stri Vectin', an anti-ageing cream to rival botox.

GREAT FOR:
Skincare, hair-care, make-up

rescu.com.au

AUS

HOME-BASED BEAUTY SPOT

Rescu is an e-store devoted to beauty. Featuring make-up, skincare, fragrances and bath/body treats, the site is a self-described 'sweet salvation for the beauty obsessed'. Products are neatly separated into 'The Essentials', 'Sensitive Soul', 'Make-up' and 'Bride to Be'. Purchases can also be made by brand, many of which are not readily available elsewhere in Australia, including Caudalie (France) and Joey (New York). An excellent glossary section helps decipher some of the techno-babble associated with many modern beauty products.

GREAT FOR:
Skincare, fragrances, make-up

sephora.com

USA

INNOVATIVE INTERNATIONAL BEAUTY CHAIN

Recognised as one of the leading retail beauty chains in Europe and the United States, Sephora offers what it describes as the largest and most diverse range of international beauty products available online. Classic skin- and body-care names sit alongside hard-to-find limited editions in product ranges including 'Make-up', 'Skin-care', 'Fragrance', 'Bath/Body', 'Hair' and 'Smile'. Many products can be purchased at significantly cheaper prices than presently available in Australia. Current best-sellers include Du Wop Lip Venom and Rosebud salve.

GREAT FOR:
Skincare, make-up, body-care

soulscents.org USA

LUSH BEAUTY LOTIONS & POTIONS

Sugar smoothies and skin sorbet? These are just two of the products featured at Soul Scents. Established by a massage therapist, the range combines effective skin formulas with delicious scents and inspirational packaging. There are treats for your body, face, feet and hair, including the Soothe Your Soul Foot Butter and the Salt Shaker Dead Sea Bath Salts. And back to the sorbet, don't miss the Raspberry Truffle skin sorbet, a blended shea butter and sugar salt that is a rumoured favourite of television's *Desperate Housewives*.

GREAT FOR:
Skincare, body-care, essential oils

spacenk.com UK

CUTTING-EDGE BEAUTY BOUTIQUE

Space NK is recognised as one of London's best boutiques for high-quality, innovative beauty products. With over 60 specialist brands, this online store reflects the uncluttered character of Space NK's bricks-and-mortar outlets. Buyers can shop by brand or category, including aromatherapy, fragrance, skincare and gifts. The site also provides an edited view of current make-up looks and trends. Some of the more impressive products include eye therapy patches (an instant pick-me-up for tired eyes) by Talika, Erbaviva stretch mark oil, and Expressions eau de toilette – a unisex fragrance from Space NK's signature range.

GREAT FOR:
Make-up, body-care, gifts

strawberrynet.com

USA

GREAT FOR:
Skincare, make-up, fragrances

TOP BRANDS AT A DISCOUNT

The team at StrawberryNet truly encourage the international shopper. The incredible range of discounted skincare, make-up, cosmetics and fragrances combined with free worldwide shipping make it an irresistible online destination. All the majors are there, including Clarins, La Mer, Estée Lauder and Max Factor, together with some more boutique-style labels and products. A currency converter easily converts all price listings to your local currency.

swaddlespa.com

USA

GREAT FOR:
Body-care, bathing products

SPOIL YOURSELF

I know, I know, another spa site! Swaddle, however, is a cut above many, offering a selection of natural yet decadent bath and body products combining natural butters, herbs and oils. The bathing range includes cocoa butter and sea salt chocolate truffles – promising a calorie-free bathing experience – while handcrafted soaps are available in a variety of scents including citrus sage and orange blossom ylang ylang. Herbal bath teas are also featured, together with Pucker Up lip balm made from the finest natural oils and butters and scented in sweet orange, peppermint or coconut lime.

thebodybakery — USA

BATH & BODY DESSERTS

Founder Lisa Schmoldt started this company four years ago with a mission to offer fresh, fun and unique bath and body products. The result is the Body Bakery, a line of delicious (and calorie-free) bath and body desserts including 'Whipped Cream' moisturiser, the angel cake scented 'Body & Hair Icing', and the 'Cupcake Conditioner'. Gift sets include the 'Snowflake Sampler' with four mini whipped cream moisturisers in the festive scents of 'Egg Nog', 'Gingerbread Man', 'Hot Cocoa' and 'Holiday Cookies'.

GREAT FOR:
Body creams, soaps

thisworks.com — UK

CONTEMPORARY AROMATHERAPY

Started by a former beauty director of Vogue magazine, together with the respected Aromatherapy Associates, This Works marks an exciting new direction in aroma products. Forget any New Age clichés, this site is crisp and modern, with products clearly separated into categories including bath and shower and, even, hot stone burners – an alternative to the traditional oil burner. A top seller is the fast-track travel bag with eight essential miniature products especially for travelling.

GREAT FOR:
Body-care, bathing products

ticklemywickle.com   UK

WELL-DESIGNED, MODERN NOSTALGIA

The name alone makes this site worthy of inclusion. Fortunately though, the product range of Wickle is equally irreverent and impressive. The range includes perfume, toiletries and candles. The limited edition perfumes are available in four scents: Chestnut & Vetiver, Muskmallow, Periwinkle and Scented Tea Leaf. The current collection is presented in stunning glass bottles adorned with pure silver silhouette pendants. A great range of slightly off-the-wall gifts, including designer sewing kits and vintage button sets, is also available.

GREAT FOR:
Fragrances, candles, gifts

winkbeauty.com   USA

FUN, FAST & SOPHISTICATED BEAUTY

Wink is sexy, sassy and sophisticated. Founded in 2003 by two beauty writers, the site features a beauty range for the eyes, lips, face and nails. With the hot pink and black colour palette of the site, the products are bold and ballsy and include the all-in-one mascara/eye liner duo available in one colour – 'Bad Ass Black'. For irresistibly kissable lips, look at the lip liner/gloss duos featuring a sponge tip applicator available in five shades. Shopping categories move from the 'First Date' range to the 'Take Me Home' collection.

GREAT FOR:
Make-up

a woman's wardrobe

FASHION, HANDBAGS & OTHER ACCESSORIES FOR WOMEN

agnesb.com

FR

UNCOMPLICATED FRENCH STYLE

You don't have to be French to appreciate the casual Parisian chic of Agnès B. This e-store boasts an inspirational collection of shirts, skirts, jackets, coats and dresses, which are modern yet effortlessly elegant. From a basic white shirt to a faux fur ¾ length coat, Agnès B has all the fashion requirements covered. The store also carries a select range of signature belts, hats and watches. Men's and children's collections are also available.

GREAT FOR:
Shirts, tees, jackets, accessories

anyahindmarch.co.uk

UK

HANDBAG HEAVEN

With 30 stores across the world, Anya Hindmarch is Britain's handbag high priestess. Browse through the collection for classic bags with a twist and an innovative mix of colours and textures. In celebration of the opening of the first Anya Hindmarch store in London, the Bespoke Ebury bag was introduced. Made to order in calf leather or matt crocodile, the bag is available in seven colours and two sizes. A secret message, in your handwriting, is then embossed into the inner lining of the bag. The label also pioneered personalised images transposed on to a bag with their 'Be a Bag' line.

GREAT FOR:
Handbags

bedheadpjs.com
USA

BEDWEAR WITH ATTITUDE
Sure the Garfield bed-shirt was great, but that was 1985 and it's time to move on. Bed Head is a great place to start updating your nighttime attire - and you can even wear Garfield for the very last time while you shop. The site offers bedwear with attitude. Visit for quality cotton pjs, luxe Mandarin-style robes and designer loungewear available in an impressive range of fabrics including toiles, polka dots and black lace designs. New styles include the Louis XIV pique and rosebud patterns. There are lots of celebrity endorsements in the 'Press & Exposure' section.

GREAT FOR:
Designer pjs & sleepwear

blaec.com
USA

CALIFORNIAN FASHION LEADER
Enjoy hassle-free shopping without claustrophobic change rooms or bad lighting, thanks to the online e-store of a popular Californian fashion boutique of the same name, Blaec. Launched in 1999, the site abounds with top-line international fashion apparel and accessories. Big names sit aside some emerging designers destined for bigger things. Shop by designer, listed alphabetically on the left-hand side of the screen, including Paper Denim & Cloth and Lotta, together with Australia's own Willow and Sass & Bide.

GREAT FOR:
Clothing, accessories

bluefly.com

USA

DESIGNER NAMES AT A DISCOUNT

'Over 350 designers. Up to 50% off.' That's the tantalising promise from Bluefly. Stocking clothing and accessories from more than 350 designers, you'd be hard pressed to find better priced fashion merchandise elsewhere online. With new styles introduced almost daily, it pays to regularly log in and check the collections. From Celine to Diesel, Marc Jacobs to Prada, you'll find jackets, denim, pants, tops and accessories. Look out for 'Deal a Day' promotions for even better deals on already greatly reduced merchandise.

GREAT FOR:
Clothing, handbags, shoes

candccalifornia.com

USA

CHIC T-SHIRT COLLECTIONS

According to this site, 'happiness is a C & C T-shirt'. If you're one to get excited over chic cotton tops and tees you'll love this e-store. The products are divided into 'Women', 'Men', 'Kids' and 'Sale' items or, if you prefer, you can shop purely by colour. T-shirt styles include v-neck, round neck, short- or long-sleeved. A collection of sexy tops with colourful prints is also available, complemented by coordinating fleece shirts and cotton pants. A maternity collection is also included.

GREAT FOR:
T-shirts, tops

elissabloom.com

USA

A BAG FOR EVERY STATE OF MIND

After being 'discovered' by über-retailer Bloomingdales, Elissa Bloom launched her namesake handbags and accessories collection in 2002. The online catalogue on her site promises a bag for every mood, including the mindsets of 'Sophisticated', 'Fun' and 'Elegant'. Items can also be purchased by collection – from the flirty 'Girl Collection' to the more sophisticated 'Herringbone'. Super stylish baby bags are also available.

GREAT FOR:
Handbags

eluxury.com

USA

IF YOU HAVE THE MEANS, THEY HAVE THE MERCHANDISE

The name says it all really – this site is recognised as the internet's premiere luxury retail destination. The women's ready-to-wear range is a definite highlight, featuring more than 30 international labels. Shop by brand or category, including cashmere, dresses, denim, pants and swimwear. The store has many online exclusives from names such as Louis Vuitton, Fendi and La Perla, allowing you to purchase the latest looks in the privacy of your own home. Items in the 'Sale' section are available at up to 40% off recommended retail prices.

GREAT FOR:
Clothing, accessories, perfume

figleaves.com
UK/USA

MULTI-BRAND INTIMATES
Dispelling the myth that the British can't do sexy, Figleaves is one of the world's largest intimate apparel retailers. Their e-store features no less than 250 brands and over 30,000 lingerie, sleepwear, activewear and hosiery products. All the big names are represented, including Calvin Klein, Moschino, Playtex and Wonderbra. Shop by brand, size or department or via the seasonal sale section. Specialty ranges include bridal wear, maternity and lingerie for the fuller figured. Oh, and men aren't completely forgotten – Figleaves offers an equally fashionable men's collection.

GREAT FOR:
Lingerie, underwear

flatteringflops.com
USA

DESIGNER LADIES SANDALS
Flip flops (or thongs) meet fashion at this site. The brainchild of a former NYC Fashion Institute of Technology graduate, Flattering Flops features a range of stylish yet functional summer footwear adorned with ribbons, bows and crystals. The flip flops themselves are made from 100% Brazilian rubber and are available with a classic, wedge, or kitten heel. You can also customize your own 'flops' for a truly unique design.

GREAT FOR:
Designer thongs

gap.com USA

AMERICAN FASHION ALL ROUNDER

An American fashion icon, in recent years Gap has taken a dressier turn, particularly in its women's range. Velvet jackets, textured tops and slim-line pants feature in the current collection, together with jeans available in a multitude of fits and styles. Rest assured, however, the popular classics including T-shirts, activewear and sleepwear remain, as well as a selection of bags, shoes and belts. Don't leave the site without browsing through the 'Sale' section for some great end-of-season bargains.

GREAT FOR:
Shirts, jackets, accessories

getbirdinhand.com USA

KISS NECK PAIN GOODBYE & STILL BE FASHIONABLE

'Large enough for a laptop, yet shallow enough so your keys won't get lost.' That's how founder Rachel Lincoln describes her range of exclusive Bird in Hand bags. The bags feature side pockets, which are perfectly sized for mobile phones or sunglasses. There's also a large zippered pocket on one side of the inside of the bag and a snap pocket on the other. Available in a number of colours, the bags feature patterned fabric linings. Oh, and your neck and back will thank you – Bird in Hand bags are designed to be worn as a clutch or carried in the crook of your arm.

GREAT FOR:
Handbags

johnsmedley.co.uk
UK

GREAT FOR:
Knitwear

LUXURY DESIGNER KNITWEAR

In the Fashion Kingdom there's knitwear and then there's John Smedley knitwear. The Smedley name is synonymous with luxurious cashmere and lightweight knits in classic styles and colours. The 'To Your Wardrobe' collection features a selection of iconic pieces including pure merino scoop-necked sweaters, fitted cardigans and luxury cashmere turtlenecks. For a more modest Smedley touch, take a peak at the range of lightweight wool and cashmere scarves. The site also includes great product care advice.

katespade.com
USA

GREAT FOR:
Handbags, leather accessories

ALL HAIL THE HANDBAG QUEEN

Acclaimed worldwide for her creatively chic range of handbags and accessories, New York's handbag queen Kate Spade invites you to browse her World of Beautiful Bags via this online store. Featuring more than 40 signature items including shoulder bags, totes, purses, wallets and clutches, designs are available in a range of fashionable fabrics including boldly patterned cottons, leather, straw and simple nylons. The collection of coordinated shoes is also a guaranteed style hit. Baby items, stationery pieces and a men's range by Jack Spade are also available.

laylagrace.com — USA

HIP DETAILS FOR WOMEN

Style and quality are the key words at Layla Grace. Promising to be functional, yet never mainstream, you'll find women's clothing, aprons, pjs, robes and more. Whilst the humble apron may appear somewhat staid, the Layla Grace collection includes modern, fashionable aprons, specifically crafted for the domestic goddess within – think lively colours, flirty cuts and vintage-style prints. Move into the bedroom and you'll ooh and ahh over a collection of flirty long-sleeved pjs and luxurious satin robes. The 'Home' and 'Children's' ranges are also worth a peek.

GREAT FOR: Clothing, accessories

manhattanportage.com — USA

HOME OF THE ORIGINAL NEW YORK MESSENGER BAG

With the retail philosophy to create 'a bag for everyone', Manhattan Portage boasts a fresh, innovative range of bags in all shapes and sizes. Styles include messenger bags, backpacks, laptop bags and shoulder bags. All bags are made of virtually indestructible nylon, and certain styles are lined with industrial quality nylon for extra durability. With adjustable shoulder straps, the bags are made in a number of colours including black, pink, grey, orange and red. 'New Arrivals' includes accessory cases, perfect for cameras, iPods and mobile phones.

GREAT FOR: Handbags, luggage

mycatwalk.com.au AUS

WHERE ALL THE BIG NAMES MEET
A premier online fashion boutique, My Catwalk showcases a great selection of local and international designers. The site features detailed photographs and product descriptions, together with international size-chart details. Browse through an almost never-ending range of apparel including tops and knits, jeans and pants, skirts and dresses, knitwear, coats and underwear. Finish off with a peek at the accessories range starring shoes, handbags, belts and sunglasses. A 'Member's Room' offering one-off, weekly and monthly specials is coming soon.

GREAT FOR:
Clothing, accessories

mysweetfeet.com.au AUS

FOOTWEAR WITH SEX APPEAL
The brainchild of a talented mother-and-daughter team, this Australian e-store features a range of fabulous slipper-style footwear for in and outside the house. An international hit with celebrities such as Nicole Kidman and Cate Blanchett, the current collection includes the baby blue 'Treasure Tina', the pink gingham 'Precious Pamela', and the quilted black satin 'Chic Chez'. Each pair of slippers is beautifully packed in a signature storage box. New season styles will include leopard-print and velvet designs.

GREAT FOR:
Slippers

mytote.com
USA

A PLACE FOR EVERYTHING

This label began, in part, after an embarrassing airport security check where co-founder Lisa Mathis' personal effects were exposed for all her fellow travellers to see. The result was a range of fashionable totes perfect for organising your belongings at home or on the road. The e-store offers items such as the 'Chamberlain Standard Tote', a two-pocket, fully lined tote with individual areas for shoes and accessories. There's also the 'Chamberlain Swim Tote', the 'Madison Make-up Bag' and the 'Aasha Travel Kit'. All designs are available in an impressive range of unique fabrics.

GREAT FOR:
All purpose bags

nealdecker.com
USA

HANDMADE FEW-OF-A-KIND BAGS

A great handbag has always been a fashion necessity and the range by Neal Decker is exceptional. Handmade in New York City, the range features Italian leather and brass detailing. Many of the items are limited editions and made to order, which merely adds to their allure. Four core styles are available – Slouch, Town & Country Tote, Porthole and Slim. Bags are available in a variety of colours and fabrics including chocolate, tangerine and olive, and in vintage cloths and trims.

GREAT FOR:
Handbags

net-a-porter.co.uk

UK

GREAT FOR:
Clothing, accessories

GLOBAL FASHION BOUTIQUE

Perhaps the most famous top-end e-store, Net-a-Porter is designed to provide the best in designer clothing, bags, shoes and accessories. Magazine-style in its look and layout, the store is easy to shop in and incredibly well stocked. Search by categories including 'Product Type' (e.g. clothing) or 'Designer', as well as 'Runway' collections with items straight from the international fashion shows. Perfect gifts for the fashionista/s in your life are also available, with treats including jewellery, belts and bags. Most orders are delivered in signature black boxes with coordinating ribbon.

oliverandcoco.com.au

AUS

GREAT FOR:
Handbags, luggage

HANDBAGS & ACCESSORIES FOR ALL-OVER STYLE

Who knew that such great bags were right on our doorstep? With a signature range of totes, overnight bags and cosmetic cases, Oliver & Coco combines style with sensibility. Items are available in a range of colours and materials including nylon, leather and canvas. The bags are very Longchamp in style, but for a fraction of the cost. My 'Overnighter' in continental beige has proved the perfect travelling companion, while a chocolate, leather-handled tote has served as a great all-rounder. Orders can also be placed by phone, and a mackintosh and men's range is planned.

p45.com
USA

ONE OF CHICAGO'S BEST
An online fashion boutique, p45 stocks an innovative collection of women's clothing and accessories. Regularly listed as one of Chicago's hottest fashion destinations, young designers are well represented in the p45 range, which is clearly separated into departments including 'Tops', 'Bottoms', 'Dresses' and 'Shoes'. Featured labels include Flavio Olivera and Beth Bowley. Great profiles of featured designers are included and 'In the News' provides magazine extracts on some of the brands stocked.

GREAT FOR:
Clothing, accessories

peepaccessories.com
USA

ACCESSORIES FOR CHICKS
The girls at Peep sell 'accessories for chicks'. More specifically they offer a fresh and innovative collection of one-of-a-kind handbags and limited-edition accessories. Each item is handmade and can be truly described as wearable and useable art. In 'Bags', browse through unique handbags, clutches, evening bags, wallets and totes, while the 'Etc' department has a great line of scarves, jewellery, and even iPod cosies. A custom design service is also available. Find out what other shoppers have to say about the store in the 'Peepers' section on the site.

GREAT FOR:
Handbags, accessories

peteralexander.com.au — AUS

DESIGNER AUSSIE SLEEPWEAR

No-one does cool sleepwear quite like Peter Alexander. Browse this online boutique for pj sets, sleepwear separates, nighties and intimates in tropical prints, bold patterns and witty quips. Cashmere-blend gowns and coordinated slippers complete the look. For underwear with some attitude, take a look at the five-pack 'Lucky Knickers' box set of cotton spandex underpants with diamante detailing. Sexy silk nighties in sunshine and lemonade shades are also available. Men's and kid's collections are also featured, together with a collection of gifts categorised according to price.

GREAT FOR: Sleepwear, leisure wear

poshbytori.com — USA

HANDBAGS FOR A FABULOUS LIFE

According to designer Tori Alvarado, Posh Handbags is 'all about life – a fabulous life'. This e-store showcases an original collection of bags ranging from an envelope clutch to an urban city tote. The featured fabrics are equally eclectic and include stunning silk brocade, candy stripes and classic black and white polka dots. The range includes the more practically focused baby/travel bags and laptop totes. Coordinated fabric sashes can be purchased here, and worn as belts or headscarves. The site abounds with testimonials from heaps of happy customers.

GREAT FOR: Handbags

purseket.com
USA

DIG IN YOUR GARDEN & NOT YOUR BAG
World hunger, global warming, international conflict, finding something from the depths of your handbag – at least one of these pressing issues can be solved by the team at Purseket. You see, Purseket make an ingenious product – a removable set of portable fabric pockets for storing your make-up, sunglasses, phone or wallet, easily removable from totes, travel bags and beach bags. Available in a range of colours and sizes, you're sure to find a purseket to suit your needs. I now live by the purseket motto: 'dig in your garden and not your purse'.

GREAT FOR:
Storage pockets

ronherman.com
USA

BEVERLY HILLS STATUS & SOPHISTICATION
Ron Herman caters for those seeking 'style, status and sophistication'. His recently launched e-commerce site features a suitably slick range of women's dresses, jeans, lingerie, tops and accessories. Stocked labels include Citizens of Humanity, Emilio Pucci and Marc Jacobs. Click onto the 'Press' section for glimpses of today's hottest names decked out in this season's must-have items from this iconic retailer. A range of international music is also available including the exclusive 'Ron Herman' signature CD.

GREAT FOR:
Clothing

rupertsanderson.co.uk

UK

HANDCRAFTED SHOES & LUGGAGE

Rupert Sanderson is passionate about the craft of shoe-making. Spending four months of the year in Italy, he designs for a number of high-end fashion labels, as well as his own range of sophisticated shoes. The current collection has a distinct Carnaby Street feel, with shiny buckles and rounded toes. An equally gorgeous range of made-to-order luggage has also been added and includes a small collection of cases and bags in bleached kid leather with edging available in 22 colours. Certainly not the cheapest pieces, but think of them as a travelling investment.

GREAT FOR: Shoes, luggage

shopbop.com

USA

BOUTIQUE SHOPPING MADE EASY

When the thought of trudging from boutique to boutique is too much to bare, try stopping by Shopbop. You'll find designer accessories, basic tees, cashmere, denim, dresses and pants. Each product includes an informative description and a double-click function for a close-up of each item. Leading fashion names such as Diesel, Diane von Furstenberg and Juicy Couture all make an appearance, together with some not-so-high-profile, but equally impressive names. Excellent bios of new brands are worth a read, as is the 'What's New' collection featuring exciting new store arrivals.

GREAT FOR: Clothing, accessories

shopintuition.com — USA

HOLLYWOOD'S HOTTEST ONLINE

At Shop Intuition, all roads lead to fashion. The latest, coolest and most sought-after fashion, to be precise. With halter dresses, vintage jeans and braided belts, the site is a self-described 'general store for fashionistas'. Click on 'As Seen In' for the store's wares in a predominantly Hollywood context, and take a look at 'What's New' for the latest arrivals. And your pampered pet isn't forgotten – the store has a super chic collection of designer dog accessories including dog bone necklaces and couture pet carriers.

GREAT FOR: Clothing, accessories

shopkitson.com — USA

A CELEBRITY FAVOURITE

Ever wondered where Hollywood starlets get their great tees and bags? Chances are its Kitson on LA's hip Robertson Boulevard. With a commitment to finding the newest and hottest, this e-store showcases a range of Kitson merchandise including tops, tees, cosmetics, books and handbags. You'll find labels such as L.A.M.B., Curious George and Dirty Diamond alongside Creed fragrances. Look out for the exclusive signature Kitson tees including the now famous 'Team Aniston' and 'Team Jolie' range in honour of the recent Brad 'n' Jen Hollywood split.

GREAT FOR: Designer tees, handbags

spanx.com
USA

PROBLEM-SOLVING PANTIES

At Spanx it's all about creating the best impression, thanks to a unique range of ultra flattering hosiery, body-shaping bodysuits and slimming apparel. The label has literally re-shaped the lives (and bodies) of women all over the world with its patented designs, which include footless tummy control tights, mid-thigh shapers, seamless bras and the new 'Bod a Bing' v-neck top. Maternity and plus-size items are also available.

GREAT FOR:
Hosiery, slimming apparel

standardstyle.com
USA

BOUTIQUE WITH A FLAIR FOR FASHION

This website aims to bring together the very best in international fashion and accessories for men, women and children – a 'fashion forward boutique for the chic'. For women the store is especially good, neatly combining cutting-edge style and casual classics. Shop by label or product category. 'What's New' showcases new arrivals with great photographs and clear merchandise descriptions. A hip maternity collection, together with beauty and body gifts, is also available.

GREAT FOR:
Clothing, accessories

theclearbox.com

NZ/UK

THE BEST WAY TO STORE EVERYTHING

Wardrobe a shambles? Look no further than this e-store for a stylish yet practical range of, you guessed it, clear boxes. Boxes are available in sizes perfect for shoes, boots, handbags and scarves. All items come flat-packed and are available in crystal clear, tantalising turquoise, powder-puff pink and luscious lilac. Most boxes can be purchased in packs of three or 10 but, from experience, I can guarantee that once you start, you won't be able to stop. New arrivals include hat boxes, together with multi-purpose storage boxes suitable for everything from T-shirts to toys.

GREAT FOR:
Storage products

---

thelaundress.com

USA

LUXURIOUS LAUNDERING

Who says laundering can't be stylish? Certainly not The Laundress, an innovative e-store showcasing a selection of products to create a luxuriously pleasurable experience out of a necessary chore. The collection incorporates a range of exclusive detergents and fabric care products, including a best-selling wool and cashmere shampoo and a crease-release spray, together with embroidered drawstring bags in a range of sizes. Make sure you read through the 'Recipes' section for some great laundry tips.

GREAT FOR:
Laundry accessories

threadcountzzz.com
USA

COMFORT AWAKE OR ASLEEP
Thread Count (zzz) promises the ultimate in luxurious comfort for sleeping, lounging and relaxing. For women, browse through the collection of Egyptian cotton sleepwear embroidered with beautiful dragonflies and dyed-to-match shell buttons. Also take a peek at the 'Ribbon' range of pjs and coordinated gowns in a variety of colours. All pjs are packaged with matching mini-pillowcases. Men's and travel collections are also available.

GREAT FOR:
Sleepwear, loungewear

toryltd.com
USA

THE SOPHISTICATED MANHATTAN WARDROBE
A well-kept secret amongst New York's best dressed, Tory Ltd is the brainchild of fashion public relations veteran Tory Burch. Her sophisticated collection has a distinctive 1960s and '70s feel and includes a stunning range of tailored tunics available in velvet, suede and cotton. Complete the Tory look with a selection of unique shoes, belts, handbags and jewellery. The 'Resort Collection' proves that fashion standards don't need to drop when hitting the beach. It includes super drawstring pants, cotton tanks and lightweight tops.

GREAT FOR:
Clothing, accessories

victoriassecret.com

USA

UNDERWEAR TOO BEAUTIFUL TO HIDE

There's underwear and then there's Victoria's Secret. Synonymous with the sexiest bras, panties and sleepwear, there's a range to suit any style. Together with Victoria's signature collections, designer labels including Chantal Thomass and Spoylt also have starring roles. Purchases can also be made by product type and even I was shocked by the plethora of undergarments available. Let the Victoria's Secret look continue throughout your wardrobe with a clothing range featuring cashmere tops, designer jeans and evening attire.

GREAT FOR: Lingerie, sleepwear

vivre.com

USA

A CELEBRATION OF LUXURY & DELIGHT

It doesn't get much more luxurious than Vivre, an e-store committed to providing its customers with what it describes as a 'meticulously edited collection of the world's finest selections'. Whilst ranges for men, kids and the home are available, the women's range is where the site really excels. Flip through the 'Holiday Essentials' for cashmere sweaters and satin slingbacks or 'Forever Collectibles' for a chiffon tunic and reversible shrug. Handbags from style leaders Michael Kors, Vera Wang and Roberto Cavelli are also on show, together with an immaculate selection of sleepwear, lingerie and jewellery.

GREAT FOR: Clothing, homewares

wellies.co.nz
NZ

DESIGNER GUMBOOTS

Who would have thought that the humble gumboot could be re-invented as a fashion essential. Forget boring black and welcome the decidedly more snappy palette of green, pink, yellow and baby blue at this e-store featuring the acclaimed 'Hunter' boots. They are the only gumboots to incorporate a latex-dipped inner lining for extra durability and, perhaps more importantly, are available in great fashion forward colours. A new range of boots featuring floral designs is also available, as is the 'Galloway' range, described as 'next generation' gumboots.

GREAT FOR:
Gumboots

witchery.com.au
AUS

CLASSIC AUSTRALIAN DAYWEAR

At Witchery it's all about the simple, stylish wardrobe, with a distinctly modern twist. Visit their e-store for beaded singlets, printed tanks and scoop tops, as well as denim skirts, cropped pants and slim-fit trousers. The label's exclusive range of accessories including jewellery, handbags, totes and purses can also be purchased online. Click onto 'Underwear' for their popular undergarments including the seamless singlet. A 'Shoe Collection' completes the range.

GREAT FOR:
Clothing, accessories

the male room

CLOTHING & ACCESSORIES FOR THE MEN IN YOUR LIFE

aspinaloflondon.com

UK

PURE BRITISH ELEGANCE

For fine leather goods and accessories, look no further than this store. Aspinal of London is renowned for its impeccable range of leather diaries, address books, briefcases, photo frames and travel accessories – all handmade using traditional leather and bookbinding methods. In addition to the classic blacks and browns, most items are also available in contemporary shades of pink, blue, red and purple. All leather books are individually hand-coloured and polished, enhancing the depth of colour, texture and tone. Most items can be stylishly personalised with engraving in gold, silver or blind embossing.

GREAT FOR:
Briefcases, diaries, travel accessories

ctshirts.co.uk

UK

QUALITY ENGLISH SHIRT MAKERS

The team at Charles Tyrwhitt (pronounced Tirrit!) aim to 'surprise, delight and excite' with a superb collection of quality men's shirts, ties, cufflinks, suits and shoes. Combining quality fabrics with styles including fitted cut-away, button-down and evening designs, all CT shirts are cut for style and comfort, with a variety of sleeve lengths and pearl-style buttons. A range of silk ties completes this well-dressed picture, together with socks, nightwear and grooming sets.

GREAT FOR:
Shirts, accessories

egentlemen.com

USA

SKINCARE, SHAVING & GROOMING

With a focus on high-end 'real' men's grooming supplies, eGentlemen is a one-stop shop for a man who enjoys and values the concept of personal care. Products are separated into 'Shave', 'Body', 'Face' and 'Hair' categories, together with a section devoted to ready-made grooming kits including shaving kits and men's travel kits. Stocked brands include Decleor, eShave and The Art of Shaving. An 'Advice' section is also included, providing helpful information on shaving, grooming and skin care.

GREAT FOR:
Body-care, shaving products, hair-care

forzieri.com

IT

FINE ITALIAN LEATHERGOODS

The internet retail division of a premier Italian-based leather and luxury goods company, Forzieri features an impressive collection of predominantly handmade items. For men you'll find silk cashmere scarves, smooth leather belts, gloves, hats and even leather jackets. There are also some exquisite wallets, silver giftware and watch cases. Together with signature Forzieri pieces, stocked brands include Alessi, Rita Botta and RG House of Florence. A 'Gift-Finder' facility helps narrow down the right gift for any occasion.

GREAT FOR:
Wallets, scarves, cashmere sweaters

hawesandcurtis.com

UK

DISTINGUISHED BRITISH MENSWEAR

Sure they may not be too great at cricket or boast any recent swimming champs, but the British sure know how to do classic menswear. This site is the online presence of distinguished menswear company Hawes & Curtis and features a 'Formal Range', 'Fashion Range', ties and cufflinks. The formal range includes pure cotton shirts in a variety of plain, textured and patterned fabrics, while in the fashion range you'll find more contemporary and fitted designs in a variety of colours and styles. Acollection of cufflinks is also available, together with a stylish women's range.

GREAT FOR:
Shirts, ties, cufflinks

hermes.com

USA/FR

EXCLUSIVE FRENCH FASHION HOUSE

If you've got the means, then Hermes has the merchandise. The e-store of this iconic luxury French retailer showcases a range of merchandise including ties, scarves and fragrances. Once you've selected a tie you can view it close up or even try it on with a shirt. Whilst the entire Hermes collection is not currently available online, the site does include a selection of women's scarves and bracelets, as well as top-end baby gifts including a cashmere hat and mittens set.

GREAT FOR:
Ties, cashmere scarves, fragrances

herringbone.com.au — AUS

TAILORED SHIRTS & ACCESSORIES

Australia's Herringbone is 'distinguished by detail'. Founded in Sydney in 1997, the company produces an outstanding collection of boutique-style men's shirts, ties and cufflinks. The shirt range includes classic collars, slim-fit and tuxedo styles, all available in a variety of colours and patterns including blue, pink and white. You can even choose whether or not your shirt has a pocket, and customise your sleeve length. Accessories include exclusive ties, rhodium-plated cufflinks, shoes and swim shorts. A custom design service is also available, as well as a collection of Herringbone shirts for women.

GREAT FOR: Shirts, ties, cufflinks

intimo.com — USA

LUXE MEN'S UNDERWEAR & SLEEPWEAR

Look as good with your clothes off as you do with them on, or so goes the simple philosophy from the team at Intimo. Integrating fashion with function, the range features designer men's underwear and sleepwear including boxers, briefs, long johns and cashmere robes. The 'Gift Shop' showcases a collection of gifts for men of any age. There's also a women's range featuring designer lingerie, hosiery, pjs and robes.

GREAT FOR: Underwear, pjs

itsaboything.co.nz
NZ

GADGETS, GIZMOS & GIFTS FOR MEN

A New Zealand-based family business, this e-store can help with the often daunting task of selecting the perfect gif for the man or men in your life. With five distinct categories – 'Accessories', 'Grooming', 'Gadgets', 'Games' and 'Unique' – you'll find everything from underwear and shaving products to binoculars and a deluxe chess set. The featured merchandise, whilst modest, has obviously been carefully selected.

GREAT FOR:
Underwear, grooming products, games

jcrew.com
USA

ICONIC AMERICAN SPORTSWEAR

An international brand known for its range of sophisticated classics to 'live, work, play, and get married in', the J. Crew e-store features an exceptional clothing collection including men's sweaters, knits, tees, suits and accessories. A selection of limited edition items is also available, with current items including cashmere v-necks and velvet sports coats. You can make your clothing even more personal with a classic monogram service. The 'Wedding Shop' showcases a collection of traditional wedding apparel including tuxedos, suits and dinner jackets.

GREAT FOR:
Knitwear, shirts, ties, sleepwear

landsend.com
USA

THE CASUAL CLOTHING COMPANY
An 'early adaptor' of the internet, Land's End launched its website in 1995 showcasing a line of traditionally styled clothing, homewares and luggage. Of particular significance is the store's men's collection, which includes activewear, shirts, blazers, scarves, jeans and sleepwear. A selection of very reasonably priced cashmere sweaters is available in a range of styles and colours. There's also a special 'Tall/Long'-sized line of clothing in all major categories. The site also includes 'My Virtual Model', a feature enabling you to try clothing on a model based on your personal measurements.

GREAT FOR:
Shirts, jeans, outerwear, polos

menkind.co.uk
UK

EXTRAORDINARY GIFTS FOR MEN
With the diverse range of products featured on this site, you're sure to find the perfect gift for the man who has everything. Founded in 2001 with the aim of solving the age-old problem of what to buy for men, categories include 'Style', 'Sport & Fitness', 'At Work' and 'Boys Toys', where you'll find model cars, electronic card games and innovative gadgets. New store arrivals include the 20th-anniversary Rubiks Cube and the Flavour Shaker – Jamie Oliver's modern take on the mortar and pestle. Apparel by designers French Connection, Ted Baker and Calvin Klein is also featured.

GREAT FOR:
Wallets, watches, cufflinks

mensessentials.com
CAN

MEN'S SKINCARE SPECIALISTS
This e-store is frequently referred to as the premier online destination for male grooming products. Stocking the wares of more than 25 international brands including Baxter of California and MenScience, you'll find a plethora of high-quality skincare, hair-care, shaving and sun protection products. There's also a popular 'Reading' section, which includes great grooming guides. Gift giving is made easy with a selection of kits and gift sets – the Brave Soldier Jetset Travel Box and the American Crew Great Shavings Combo are two current highlights.

GREAT FOR:
Skincare, shaving products, body-care

nickelformen.com
USA

SERIOUS SKINCARE FOR MEN
Forget a dab of sunscreen and an occasional slap of moisturiser, this store offers 'serious skin care for men'. With a range of self-described straight-talking products, the current collection includes an eye contour lift cream, facial scrubs and the morning-after rescue gel, all specially formulated for men's skin. Take a look at the popular 'Repair Kit', a red tin box filled with a selection of skin-care essentials.

GREAT FOR:
Skincare, body-care

oldnavy.com

USA

AFFORDABLE AMERICAN CLASSICS

Old Navy began more than 20 years ago with a single store in California. By 2004 the company boasted a total of 844 stores stocked with a range of modern American apparel for babies, women and men. For men you'll find denim and cords, tees, polo shirts, blazers, underwear and socks, all with a distinctly casual feel. You can also shop the 'Favourites' section for new arrivals, outfit styles and wear-to-work items. There are also designated 'Items of the Week', all offered at unbeatable prices. The 'Latest Buzz' includes all the regularly updated news from the Old Navy team.

GREAT FOR:
T-shirts, polos, sweaters

paulsmith.co.uk

UK

BRITISH FASHION'S IT BOY

Pre-eminent British designer Paul Smith comes online with this great fashion e-store. With a total of 12 collections including Paul Smith, Paul Smith Jeans, Paul Smith Accessories, most items are manufactured in England and Italy. The store is packed full of men's merchandise including shirts, jeans, knitwear, T-shirts and sleepwear. The range is completed by a selection of signature cufflinks, gloves, scarves and ties. You'll also find Paul Smith luggage, pens and men's toys including a toy 'Bluebird' land speed car and the 'Dear Cab Driver' napkins for communicating with your driver after a few too many drinks.

GREAT FOR:
Shirts, jeans, knitwear

polo.com

USA

REDEFINING AMERICAN STYLE

Hip new designers may come and go, but fashion icon Ralph Lauren continues to impress with a collection of timeless American apparel. This e-store, featuring Lauren's Polo and related ranges, is comprehensively stocked and slickly presented. Beginning more than three decades ago with a collection of men's ties, the range now includes preppy polo shirts, chinos, jeans, pants, rugby tops, sweats and tees. Search by specific items or brands within the Ralph Lauren family including Polo Jeans, Polo Golf or the Polo Shirt Shop. You'll also find sunglasses, underwear, shoes and fragrances.

GREAT FOR:
Polo shirts, sweaters, ties

racinggreen.co.uk

UK

EASY-TO-WEAR CASUALS

Over more than 15 years, Racing Green has established a well-deserved reputation for quality, well-designed menswear. Browse the site for shirts, suits, shoes and accessories. The shirt range is particularly impressive and you can shop by colour, design, cuff, collar or fabric. Once an item is selected, the site will direct you to similar or coordinating items you may be interested in. Look out for great seasonal reductions on selected items.

GREAT FOR:
Knitwear, polo shirts, T-shirts

thesharperimage.com USA

CUTTING-EDGE GADGETS & GIFTS
Packed with the latest in innovative merchandise with the promise of making life easier, The Sharper Image is a gadget guy's utopia. You'll find personal care items including massage chairs and air purifiers, state of the art MP3 players and high-end toys and travel accessories, all clearly categorised by simple product descriptions. New products include the 'Scooba Floor Washing Robot' and the ingenious 'Vincci Wine Opener' and 'Vacuum Sealer'. The site also includes an 'Outlet Store' for discounted items.

GREAT FOR:
Electronics, corporate gifts, office products

thomaspink.co.uk UK

LUXURY SHIRTS, TIES & ACCESSORIES
Lauded as one of London's leading luxury shirt makers, even the most severely style-challenged man can't go wrong on this site. With distinctive pink packaging, the Thomas Pink men's range includes shirts in a range of styles, collars and colours from the classic white evening shirt to multi-stripe casual weekend designs. The store's colour palette is equally extensive and includes shades of blue, green, pink, red and yellow. Shirts are complemented by a collection of handmade woven and printed ties featuring exclusive designs on delicate silks. Socks, cufflinks and boxer shorts are also available.

GREAT FOR:
Shirts, ties, knitwear, cufflinks

home sweet home
HOMEWARES & DÉCOR FOR YOUR ABODE

annasova.com

USA

LUXURY ORGANIC BEDDING AND LINENS

Anna Sova wears the label 'elegant radicals' with pride. Recognising the often toxic nature of many household fabrics and textiles, the company produces a range of organic eco-safe bedding, towels, drapery and paint. The luxury 'Bed Collection' boasts crisp Belgian linen, decadent silk satin jacquard sheets, natural baby alpaca quilts and eco silk bedding sets in mystic green and rich raspberry. New arrivals include the world's first 440-thread count cotton sheets and the 300-count Saraswati organic cotton sheet sets. A monogramming service is available on most items.

GREAT FOR:
Quilts, blankets, sheets, towels

armoire.com.au

AUS

FRENCH-INSPIRED HOME- & GARDENWARE

For French-inspired homewares, minus the international air ticket, consider this e-boutique. The merchandise is neatly showcased in categories including 'For the Home' and 'For the Garden'. For an even moreauthentic French design feel, consider the sophisticated collection of candelabras and provincial-style glassware. All prices are in Australian dollars and estimated delivery times are provided for each product.

GREAT FOR:
Décor items, furniture, garden accessories

beanbagchairs.com.au
AUS

BEANBAGS WITH ATTITUDE
The team at this site believe they have designed the perfect beanbag. Featuring fashionable fabrics, double stitching, industrial strength thread and heavy duty zips, their beanbags are available in a range of fabrics including cotton drill, denim, faux fur, suede and outdoor materials. Bags are also available in kiddies, regular and large sizes. Beans and removable liners can be purchased, and the site includes some helpful tips for cleaning your beanbag.

GREAT FOR:
Beanbags

bombayduck.com
UK

HOME ACCESSORIES WITH A SENSE OF FUN
Combining the functional with the frivolous, Bombay Duck stocks a self-described range of 'fabulous gifts and home interiors'. Launched in 1993, the store prides itself on offering glamorous tableware, furniture and a signature range of vintage-style chandeliers. The silver-plate dining accessories are also sure to impress and include delicate teaspoons, sugar bowls and candlesticks. You can also shop room by room using the options on the bottom of the page. There's a 'Personality Gift-Finder' feature, which takes some of the stress out of finding the perfect present.

GREAT FOR:
Furniture, décor items, gifts

bubblecreative.com.au

AUS

SIMPLY BEAUTIFUL PRINTS

You've done the re-stumping, remodelled the kitchen, and the furniture has been delivered. Now all that's left is the somewhat daunting task of choosing the artwork. Fortunately Bubble Creative can help, with its collection of contemporary and vibrant art pieces featuring photography and computer-generated designs. The site features two galleries: 'Décor' with florals, foods and abstract images, and 'Classic' with an eclectic mix of black-and-white photographs. All designs are printed to order on canvas or block mounted. Personalised photographs or designs can also be printed.

GREAT FOR: Canvas-printed or block-mounted artwork

chicstuff.com

USA

EXCLUSIVELY IMPORTED CASHMERE COLLECTION

As blankets go, nothing quite beats the luxurious softness of cashmere and at Chic Stuff you'll find a decadent collection of 100% cashmere blankets and throws in a range of fashionable shades. Stunning 4-ply cashmere blankets are available in queen and king sizes with a matching satin trim. The throws are available in 1-, 2- and 3-ply cashmere and a pashmina blend, and are a perfect luxury travel accessory. A range of shawls, scarves and baby blankets is also featured. Check out the 'Sale' section for great end-of-season reductions on selected items.

GREAT FOR: Blankets, wraps, throws

conran.co.uk
UK

GREAT FOR:
Furniture, décor items, gifts

BRITAIN'S DESIGN GURU GOES ONLINE
Britain's design guru Terence Conran comes online at this exceptional e-store. Offering over 400 products, the site is separated into 'Furniture', 'Accessories' and 'Ideas for Living'. Signature Conran pieces include exclusive furniture collections, crisp linen sheets, luxurious kimonos, desk tidies and a selection of rugs and runners.

crateandbarrel.com
USA

GREAT FOR:
Table linens, lighting, kids' décor items

CONTEMPORARY AMERICAN FURNISHINGS
Gordon and Carole Segal, with the help of a single sales associate, opened the first Crate and Barrel store way back in 1962. Today the company has more than 100 stores across the United States and continues to grow. Their chic e-store has distinct departments covering a range of price points including 'Flatware', 'Furniture', 'Table Linens', 'Bedding' and 'Gifts'. Products are clearly presented and include informative descriptions and specifications. The 'Outlet' section includes end-of-season products at 'out-of-your-mind' prices. Seasonal catalogues providing many inspirational decorating ideas can be downloaded.

cushy-cushy.com

NZ

HANDCRAFTED DESIGNER CUSHIONS

Nothing quite finishes off a sofa like well-chosen cushions, and you'll find a great collection of varied cushion designs on this site. Made from high-quality hand-dyed New Zealand wool, together with international yarns, featured styles include Bohemian, Citrus Spring and Pacific Wave, available with feather or polyester inserts. Detailed care instructions are included on the site to ensure your purchases remain pristine. A selection of ottomans can also be made to order. This is a recommended destination for unique homewares with a distinctly personal touch.

GREAT FOR:
Cushions

detango.com

USA

RETRO-INSPIRED DRINKWARE

For a unique collection of retro-style drinkware, log onto DeTango. Try the Big Swig range of tumblers available in your choice of Revolution, Pink Flamingo and Smooch designs. The Cosmo Cody is a stainless steel caddy with four signature martini glasses and large glass mixer, while the 4 Some set of classic shot glasses features great designs including 'Cabana Boy', 'Pink Elephant' and 'Hula Girl'.

GREAT FOR:
Glasses, cocktail sets

europebynet.com   USA

MODERN EUROPEAN FURNITURE FOR LESS
This e-store has a clear mission – to offer premium furnishings for less. Established in 1999, it offers the most comprehensive online range of European home furniture and accessories. Leading labels including B & B Italia, Poliform and Salvador Dali are featured and the current product range includes armchairs, bookcases and coffee tables. All product descriptions include detailed photographs and dimensions. The 'Designers Corner' has some excellent design advice and decorating tips. A measurement conversion table is also included.

GREAT FOR:
Furniture, home décor items

grahamandgreen.co.uk   UK

ECLECTIC HOMEWARES & LIFESTYLE PRODUCTS
Established in 1974 as a freestanding London store, the Graham & Green e-boutique showcases a range of exceptional gifts and home décor items. In 'Soft Furnishings' you'll find a collection of embroidered cushions and luxurious bedding featuring rich velvet quilts. The 'Kitchen & Tabletop' department includes retro-style aprons with matching oven mitts and authentic Moroccan tea-party sets. New finds include gilded letters available in large and small sizes. Browse through 'Special Offers' for an ever-changing selection of merchandise at considerably reduced prices.

GREAT FOR:
Home accessories, lighting, furniture

gumps.com

USA

SAN FRANCISCO'S FINEST

Founded in 1861, Gump's is a San Francisco retail institution boasting a collection of high-quality homewares and collectibles with a distinct East-meets-West character. The company's e-store features a comprehensive range of products including stunning hand-woven silk table runners embellished with embroidery and tassels. In 'Bed & Bath' there's some luxurious Japanese-inspired bedding with intricate motifs. Soft fringed throws and cushions complete the range. Furniture items are listed by type (e.g. tables, sofas and ottomans) and by room.

GREAT FOR:
Bedding, table linen, décor items

iggloo.co.uk

UK

CONTEMPORARY HOMEWARES WITH A RETRO FEEL

Lighting, kitchenware, furniture, tableware and bathroom accessories – they're all here at Iggloo. Shop by product or designer for some contemporary homewares including stainless steel table lamps, coordinated placemat and coaster sets, and designer scales and shower curtains. All designers are profiled, providing some interesting detail on the people behind the products. For those with a leaning toward the kitsch, the site proudly boasts a collection of truly kitsch clocks, lunch boxes, picnic bags and trays.

GREAT FOR:
Tableware, furniture, lighting

inleafdesign.com

USA

HANDCRAFTED HOME & PERSONAL ACCESSORIES

Bringing 'the wonder of nature into everyday life', In Leaf Design features a handcrafted collection of home and personal accessories including tablecloths, table napkins and tea towels. All products are made using high-quality linen or linen-cotton blends and each item is hand-printed, ensuring that no two items are exactly the same. Fig design tea towels and maple table runners are two stand-out pieces from the current collection.

GREAT FOR: Table linen, pillows, fabric bags

linenandmoore.com.au

AUS

PURE LINEN & COTTON BED LINEN

Sick of scouring the manchester aisles for quality bed and table linen at affordable prices? Then head straight to Linen and Moore, an e-store producing excellent bedding, throws, quilts and table linen. Their style is described as 'classic with a twist' and incorporates embroidered designs on crisp cotton sheets, provincial quilts, Danish-designed baby alpaca blankets and multi-coloured cushions. The 'Table Linen' collection includes quilted placemats, cotton drill napkins with coloured-stitch detailing, and a range of linen and cotton tablecloths. Beautifully embroidered hand and kitchen towels are also available.

GREAT FOR: Bedding, quilts, throws

lnt.com USA

DREAM BIG, PAY LITTLE

Linen 'n' Things encourages shoppers to dream big, but pay little. One of America's leading retailers of homewares, textiles and decorative home accessories, the company's e-store features a comprehensive product range including bedding, kitchenware, bathroom accessories, rugs and decorative accents. A great gift section selects a range of gifts tailored for recipients, including 'For Him', 'For Her' and 'For Kids'. There's also some terrific stocking-stuffers and corporate gifts. The store also presents the exclusive homewares range of Nate Berkus, Oprah Winfrey's own home décor guru. Browse 'Layered Living' for full room displays featuring stocked merchandise.

GREAT FOR: Bedding, kitchenware, home organisation

meandhugh.com AUS

CONTEMPORARY CASUAL SEATING

A Melbourne-based design company, Me and Hugh offers an exciting range of alternative seating products including the 'Sub', 'Slouch' and 'Sleeper'. A contemporary-style beanbag, the 'Slouch' is perfect for reading a book or having a nap and is available in children's styles, leather, faux fur and outdoor/water resistant designs. The 'Sleeper' is a modern take on the humble lilo and is also available in a range of colourful fabrics. The 'Sub' continues the theme and provides the perfect place to watch the world go by. All pieces require filling with polystyrene beans – a guide is sent with individual product requirements.

GREAT FOR: Beanbag-style seating

melintregwynt.co.uk — UK

PICTURE PERFECT WELSH BLANKETS

Melin Tregwynt is, in fact, a picture perfect whitewashed mill located in a wooded valley on the Welsh coast. Their online 'millshop' proudly displays a truly special collection of blankets and throws available in 'Contemporary' and 'Classic' designs. Featured colours and patterns range from dusty greys to retro-inspired spicy reds and oranges. Blankets are available from pram/cot to king bed size. A range of coordinating robes, slippers and pyjamas is also featured.

GREAT FOR: Blankets, throws

mossonline.com — USA

ICONIC SOHO DESIGN

Once described by the *New York Times* as the best design store in the United States, the online presence of this iconic Soho store is a favourite amongst design professionals and celebrities alike. There is a deliberate merging of industry and art, with an eclectic mix of products displayed side by side. Featured merchandise includes lighting, bedding, seating, office accessories and décor items. The site has a slick, contemporary feel and is easy to navigate. The 'Links' category will direct you to the sites of individual manufacturers and recommended design blogs.

GREAT FOR: Lighting, bathroom accessories, jewellery

mujionline.co.uk
UK

CONTEMPORARY JAPANESE SIMPLICITY
I have a confession to make – I am truly, madly, and deeply obsessed with this store. Since a visit to London in the early 1990s I have accumulated an ever expanding collection of Muji products, including clean and contemporary storage items, cookware, laundry items and bathroom accessories. The label originates in Japan, with Muji, according to its website, translating to 'No Brand Quality Goods'. One of my favourite items is the clear clothes pegs purchased in packs of 20. You'll also find some great travel products including canvas travel pouches, acrylic stacking pots and clear spray bottles.

GREAT FOR:
Furniture, storage, cookware, office accessories

papastour.com
UK

SCOTLAND'S FINEST MODERN ARTS & CRAFTS
Without a slither of tartan in sight, this store showcases a unique collection of more than 100 products from Scotland's contemporary craft scene. The brainchild of a leading interiors stylist, the store includes baskets, paintings, sculpture, textiles and blankets. Current 'must haves' include a Harris Tweed floor cushion with a hand-screened printed design, and a duck egg-blue and cream double-sided throw. Profiles of more than a dozen featured artists are also included. The 'Treasure Trove' features an eclectic mix of merchandise.

GREAT FOR:
Textiles, prints, blankets

pier1.com

USA

DISTINCTLY CASUAL HOMEWARES

Committed to offering customers 'distinct, casual home furnishings and décor at good value', Pier 1 Imports was founded in 1962 as a single store. Today the company boasts more than 1200 stores including this impressive e-store. Shop for furnishings, flooring, storage, ornaments and home accents including decorative cushions, throws and lighting. The store boasts that as much as 75% of each year's merchandise includes new product introductions, with many items exclusive to Pier 1. Current store catalogues can also be viewed online. The site has a particularly helpful 'Customer Relations' department.

GREAT FOR:
Furniture, home décor, storage & organisation

plushpod.com

USA

INSPIRED, AFFORDABLE MODERN FURNITURE

If you're after high-quality, modern furniture and home décor items, Plushpod has the goods. Search through 'Furniture' for modern chairs, sofas, shelving and rugs and 'Accessories' for tableware, lighting and bathroom products. Featured designers include Karim Rashid, Marc Newson and Ron Arad. The 'Sale' section showcases a great range of ever-changing merchandise.

GREAT FOR:
Furniture, storage, rugs, tableware

potterybarn.com   USA

HOME FURNISHINGS FOR COMFORT & STYLE

First up, this site has nothing to do with (a) clay or (b) animal housing. Established in 1949 as a single store in Lower Manhattan, Pottery Barn is recognised as one of America's leading homewares chains. The online presence of the company provides an opportunity to shop for a range of exclusive furniture, bedding, rugs, pillows, lighting and gifts. Shop by product type or room for coordinated furnishings and accessories. Follow the links to potterybarnkids.com and the newly established pbteen.com for homeware ranges designed specifically for teenagers.

GREAT FOR:
Bedding, tableware, home décor items

redenvelope.com   USA

SIMPLE & FUN GIFT GIVING

Launched in 1999, Red Envelope is a recognised leader in the world of gift-giving, but where it really excels is in its 'Home & Garden' range. The collection includes designer home accents, lighting, blankets and outdoor accessories, with many items exclusive to the store. All new arrivals are highlighted in the 'What's New' section and seasonal catalogues can be downloaded online. In addition to homewares, the site also has excellent gifts for him, for her, and for the kids.

GREAT FOR:
Frames, home accents, personalised gifts

replacements.com

USA

REPLACING THE IRREPLACEABLE

No witty wording or creative spiel here, this site sells exactly what it says – replacements. Or more specifically, replacement pieces of old and new china, crystal and silver. With an inventory of 10 million pieces in 200,000 patterns, items can be purchased individually to replace missing and broken items or to add to an existing collection. Stocked brands include Wedgewood, Royal Doulton and Versace. In the event that a piece or pattern you're after is not currently in stock, you can sign up to the 'Email Request Program' and be notified when your stock becomes available.

GREAT FOR:
China, crystal, silver

---

scarlettwillow.com

UK

BESPOKE PLACEMATS

To the team at Scarlett Willow, the humble placemat is like a blank canvas with no limit to the range of designs and illustrations. This e-store features a range of innovative photographic images printed on high-quality melamine-finished mats. Presented in sets of six, the placemats are available in matt or gloss finishes. Bespoke placemats are also available and can feature digital images, photographs and scannable artwork. The site promises that placemats are just the beginning, with long-term plans to embrace tableware as a whole.

GREAT FOR:
Placemats, coaster sets

shopfeatheryournest.com — USA

VINTAGE DÉCOR FOR THE HOME & GARDEN

A whimsical specialty homewares store, Feather Your Nest carries a selection of vintage-style home décor, tabletop accessories and home fragrances. Head to 'Home Accents' for unique weathered-look clocks and retro word signs, while in 'Housekeeping' you'll find Sweet Grass Farms laundry products and designer rubber gloves with pink gingham detailing. Drop by the 'Gift' department for great all-occasion gifts and gift cards by Carrot & Stick Press.

GREAT FOR:
Home accents, tableware, home fragrances

stregisathome.com — USA

FIVE-STAR FURNISHINGS

Inspired by the St Regis Beach Resort in Orange County, the collection of homewares featured on this site will bring a five-star touch to any home. You'll find imported bed linens, deluxe towels, Zen candles and exclusive tableware, all oozing with class and elegance. Complete the look with Firenze lamps and ottomans, together with contemporary ice buckets and tongs. Some items are pricey, but definitely less expensive than moving into the St Regis.

GREAT FOR:
Bedding, bathing products

thecontainerstore.com — USA

THE ORIGINAL STORAGE STORE

Lauded as 'the original storage and organisation store', The Container Store stocks a mix of products designed to simplify and organise your life. Shop for 'The Closet', 'The Home Office' and 'The Kitchen' for boxes, bins, shelves, crates, bags and trunks from an incredible range of styles and sizes. Click onto 'Savings' for some seasonal discounts. A great 'Travel' department boasts quality luggage and travel accessories.

GREAT FOR:
Wardrobe storage, shelving, home office items, travel goods

theholdingcompany.co.uk — UK

STORAGE WITH STYLE

The Holding Company promises storage with style and it more than succeeds with a collection of designer storage products for the bedroom, bathroom, kitchen and beyond. Linen rattan baskets coordinate with medong boxes to create a truly organised abode. The 'Office' section combines sensibility with style, featuring leather boxes and woven pandanus storage containers. Top sellers include the 'Breathable Wardrobe' and aluminium DVD stands.

GREAT FOR:
Baskets, storage boxes, home office accessories

thewhitecompany.com
UK

LUXURY HOMEGOODS, PREDOMINANTLY IN WHITE

White is fresh. White is new. White is timeless. The team from London's White Company know all that and offer an amazing range of home décor items and clothing, predominantly in white. Choose from luxurious cashmere throws, Roma quilts and glass ball lamps for the bedroom, together with stunning hem-stitch table linen for the dining room. Deluxe waffle towels and a signature range of soap sets are also presented. Home accessories include stylish storage boxes and exclusive home fragrance sprays. A beautiful selection of children's bedding, nightwear and nursery items is also available.

GREAT FOR:
Bedding, towels, pjs, table linen

top3.com.au
AUS

AUSTRALIA'S LEADING DESIGN STORE

Featuring the top three products in more than eight categories, Top 3 is an exciting new retail concept. All products are deemed to be the best in the world, with many the winners of international design awards. In the 'Bar & Table' department you'll find cutting-edge bottle openers, bowls and cutlery, whilst 'House & Living' boasts contemporary audio systems, clocks and lighting. The Top 3 team have even sourced chic bird feeders, dog houses and a unique white fish bowl featuring generous porthole windows. 'What's Hot' showcases new arrivals and best-selling merchandise.

GREAT FOR:
Home accessories, kitchenware, gifts

westelm.com

USA

FURNISHINGS FOR MODERN HOMES

If you've been searching for a one-stop homewares e-store, here it is. West Elm sells furniture, lighting, bedding, vases, room accents and more. Etched wall decorations and coconut curtains sit alongside textured quilts and hammered metal picture frames. A great gift department selects gifts according to price and occasion and a number of products, including towels and coasters, can be personalised.

GREAT FOR:
Furniture, wall décor, bedding

whotelsthestore.com

USA

BE A GUEST AT HOME

Five-star hotels have it all. Central locations, 24-hour room service, magically restocked mini bars and great, great, great bedding. Now you can experience crisp cotton sheets, down-filled pillows and deluxe duvets with a distinct five-star touch without checking out of home, thanks to the W Hotels e-store. For complete authenticity you can even purchase the famous W mattress made exclusively for the hotel group by Simmons. A range of bathing and home accessories is also featured including what the store describes as 'the world's best towels'.

GREAT FOR:
Bedding, throws, bathing products

words and music
BOOKS, MAGAZINES, CDs, DVDs & MORE

101cd.com

UK

THE ENTERTAINMENT MEGASTORE

A British-based online entertainment megastore, this site boasts more than 1.6 million CD, DVD and video titles. The store has a number of departments, including 'Music', 'Video' and 'Merchandise, while searches can be made by artist, title, label or track. The site also has regular sales, with many titles available at seriously reduced prices. There are also a number of 'Mini Shops' for gift buying, including 'Gifts for Teens & Kids', 'The Harry Potter Store' and 'BBC Best-sellers'. A pre-order feature is available for placing early orders for soon-to-be-released albums.

GREAT FOR:
DVDs

abebooks.com

USA

A WORLD OF BOOKS

Visit Abebooks for hard-to-find books from over 13,000 booksellers. Browse 'The Rare Book Room', 'New Books' and 'Author's Corner' for books on every conceivable subject. If more desperate measures are required, sign up for 'Book Sleuth', where you can post information on your desired book on a message board and hope someone in cyberspace can point you in the right direction. The company also has five international sites. Author profiles and interviews are also featured.

GREAT FOR:
Biographies, history, rare books

acanthuspress.com

USA

ARCHITECTURAL PUBLICATIONS

One of the world's leading publishers of fine books on residential architecture and design, Acanthus Press is a cyber treasure trove of collectable publications of impeccable quality and content. Titles can be purchased direct from the site, which also includes detailed profiles of each book. Most titles fall into one of five 'series' including 'Urban & Domestic Architecture', '20th-Century Decorators' and 'Elements of Leisure'.

GREAT FOR: Architectural books

---

alibris.com

USA

FIFTY MILLION REASONS TO SHOP

According to their site, 'you'll find it at Alibris' and, chances are, you probably will. Stocking an enviable range of over 50 million used, new and out-of-print books, the store is easy to navigate even for those new to online shopping. Search by title, artist or subject, or flip through some of the staff picks. The site also sells movies and music in almost every genre. Alibris offers a satisfaction guarantee and simple returns policy.

GREAT FOR: Non-fiction, history

amazon.com   USA

THE MARKET LEADER
The Big Kahuna of online shopping, Amazon is one of the best-known e-stores, providing the template for successful, user-friendly e-commerce. This e-store was started in 1995 and features millions of book titles including the latest releases, literary classics and used book/out-of-print titles, complemented by an impressive DVD selection. The site also includes innovative features like 'Search Inside the Book', allowing you to view sections of selected books online. Amazon also offers an excellent range of non-book merchandise, which, unfortunately, is not yet available for direct shipping to Australia.

GREAT FOR:
All books, DVDs

angusandrobertson.com.au   AUS

AUSTRALIA'S OWN
The online presence of this leading Australian bookseller is a great place to start your search for all the current best-sellers as well as special interest and children's titles. Current top 10 sellers are clearly listed, together with a brief profile of each book. 'Guaranteed Great Reads' hand-picked for your reading pleasure are featured and reviewed. You can also sign up for an email newsletter to keep you up to date with new releases and book news. Gift vouchers are also available.

GREAT FOR:
New releases, business, travel books

biblio.com
USA

FIND USED, RARE & OUT-OF-PRINT BOOKS
Bringing together more than 4000 independent booksellers from around the world, Biblio offers more than 30 million high-quality used books. You'll find out-of-print books, first editions, signed books or current best-sellers, all at competitive prices. The easy-to-use site allows you to search for a specific book by title and related details, or you can browse through books by subject, including 'Adventure & Travel', 'Art', 'Biography', 'History' and 'True Crime'. There's a 'Rare Book Room' featuring a selection of books suitable for collectors, and textbooks can also be purchased (at a stated 40% off) in the 'Textbook Warehouse'.

GREAT FOR:
Rare books, travel books

booksamillion.com
USA

FOR THE LOVE OF BOOKS
Anyone after best-sellers at discount prices should head to this store. The third-largest book-seller in the USA, Books a Million (a.k.a. BAMM) stocks all the big names, together with many hard-to-find publications. A 'Millionaires Club' discount card is available, providing 10% off all purchases for 12 months. Magazines, calendars and audio books are also available as well as a range of collectibles including stamps and vintage coins.

GREAT FOR:
Book bargains

booksontape.com

USA

UNABRIDGED BOOKS ONLINE

A division of publisher Random House Inc, Books on Tape offers an unparalleled range of book recordings for purchase on tape, CD and for download. With thousands of tapes available, you'll find all the current best-sellers, together with literary classics and popular titles. All recordings feature professionally trained actors, many of whom are house-hold names. You can search by author, title or genre, including 'Biography', 'Mystery', 'Science & Fiction' and 'Young Readers'. Not just suitable for those unable to read traditional books, books on tape are perfect for road or plane travel.

GREAT FOR:
Audio books
– classics, mystery

booktopia.com.au

AUS

BOOK BUYER'S PARADISE

With more than a million titles currently on offer, this Australian e-store claims to be the country's fastest growing online book retailer. Featured departments include 'Best-sellers' and books separated into genres including 'Art', 'Biography', 'Gardening', 'Music' and 'Technology'. For any special queries, the site features a live help chat facility. Together with many discounted prices (up to 70% of r.r.p. in the 'Bargain Books' area), the store also offers a flat Australian delivery rate of A$6.50 for up to 20 books.

GREAT FOR:
Fiction, general reference books

buyindies.com — USA

INDEPENDENT & HARD-TO-FIND FILMS

This store features a catalogue of more than 50,000 independent educational and hard-to-find films and videos on VHS, DVD and video download. Launched in 2000, the store includes film categories such as 'Animation', 'Business', 'Drama', 'Classic' and 'Comedy'. There are also listings of 'Holiday Favourites', 'Best Movies for Kids' and 'Best Short Films'. If the film you're after isn't listed you can submit your request and the team at BuyIndies can track it down for you!

GREAT FOR: Short films, animation

cduniverse.com — USA

YOUR ONLINE MUSIC SOURCE

Shopping for music online is easy thanks to e-stores like this. Flip from blues to heavy metal and even hip-hop collections, all at competitive prices. You can also buy movies, games and accessories including headphones and CD carry cases. Current musical best-sellers, new releases and top future releases are also listed. Dip into the 'Bargain Bin' for some great music, most at heavily discounted prices.

GREAT FOR: New releases, box sets

discountmagazines.com USA

MAGAZINES AT A DEEP DISCOUNT

If you're tired of paying big bucks for all the major magazine titles, click on this site for unbeatable discounted magazine subscriptions. Titles are listed alphabetically and include everything from *Architectural Digest*, *Brides*, *Cosmopolitan* and *New York* magazine to *Mac Addict* and *Men's Journal*, many starting as low as US$5.95 for 12 months. The FAQ section is clearly set out and should answer any subscription queries.

GREAT FOR:
All magazine titles

ecookbooks.com USA

COOKING CENTRAL

This e-store is where 'the world comes for cookbooks'. With more than 11,000 titles, the site boasts the world's largest cookbook range, including current best-sellers and out-of-print titles, all at substantial savings. You'll find book categories such as 'All Purpose' cookbook classics, 'Budget Cooking', 'Healthy Cooking', 'Hot & Spicy' and 'Low Carb Cooking'. There's also a 'Recipe' section featuring hundreds of great online recipes, together with a selection of cuisine-related posters. Take a look at 'Closeouts' for discounted titles at further reduced prices.

GREAT FOR:
Cookbooks

encorerecords.com — UK

RARE MUSIC FROM AROUND THE WORLD

Encore Records promises one of the largest online selections of hard-to-find, rare and collectable LPs, CDs, cassettes, videos and DVDs from around the globe. Based in the UK, all items can be shipped internationally. Make your selection by browsing through the alphabetically listed artists or by music format, including 12-inch CDs, LP promo sets and mini-discs. New arrivals are highlighted in the regularly updated 'What's New' section of the site. You'll also find a collection of promotional items including badges, displays and press packs.

GREAT FOR: Rare & collectable music

freakemporium.com — UK

MUSIC COLLECTOR'S NIRVANA

A store 'run by collectors for collectors', Freak Emporium started in 1991 as an insert inside a cult internet magazine dedicated to garage rock. From such humble beginnings the store is now a comprehensive music collector's nirvana boasting over 20,000 products. More than 90 music genres are featured, including '50s, '60s, heavy metal, jazz, rock, reggae and punk. You can pre-order selected items added to the online catalogue. A selection of music related DVDs can also be purchased.

GREAT FOR: New wave, soul/funk, progressive music

htfr.com

UK

VINYL & DJ SUPERSTORE

This e-store, Hard to Find Records, is a self-described 'DJ Superstore' selling the best vinyl and DJ equipment in the world. With over 100,000 records in stock, you can browse music genres including acid house, Detroit techno, R'n'B and trance, or look through vinyl specials including new release albums, box sets and bargain packs. DJ equipment can also be purchased by product or manufacturer.

GREAT FOR:
New vinyl, classic vinyl, DJ equipment

jbhifi.com.au

AUS

MUSIC MARKET LEADER

Hands down one of the world's best value bricks-and-mortar music stores, the online presence of JB Hi-Fi boasts an incredible range of the latest CDs, DVDs, games and digital cameras at the cheapest prices. The site is easy to navigate and all products are clearly listed – look out for JB Hi-Fi 'Staff Picks'. Featured music genres include 'Pop/Rock', 'Dance', 'Country', 'Classical' and 'Soundtracks'. Something you might not know – you can download tracks from the site, which also offers a 30-second song sample feature. A pre-order music facility is coming soon.

GREAT FOR:
Music, DVDs, games

magazinecity.net
USA

SUBSCRIPTION CENTRAL
The brainchild of a group of American magazine professionals, Magazine City promises savings on more than 1500 magazine titles from 60 major categories including 'Bridal', 'Fashion', 'Business', 'Travel', 'Cooking' and 'Men's' titles. The store also offers a range of 'Special Packages' featuring popular titles such as 'It's a Guy Thing', 'The Fashion Plate' and 'The Sporting Life'. A 'Gift Centre' provides some great gift ideas for him, for her, for parents, and more!!

GREAT FOR: Big name magazine titles

magazines.com
USA

YOUR SUBSCRIPTION HEADQUARTERS
According to its website, Magazines.com is your 'subscription headquarters'. Launched in 1996, the site offers more than 1500 consumer and business publications. The company prides itself on excellent customer service and prompt, reliable delivery. Browse through magazines by subject, title or alphabetical listing and look out for 'two for one' price deals on selected titles. Current top sellers include *In Style*, *Time* and *Oprah Magazine*.

GREAT FOR: Best-selling magazines

magshop.com.au

AUS

MAGAZINES & MORE
An online retail shop for Australia's leading magazine publishers, MagShop offers a diverse range of titles all on one easy-to-use site. All the big names are there, including the best-selling *Australian Women's Weekly*, *Australian Gourmet Traveller* and *Money Magazine*. The store also offers a wide selection of back issues for selected titles. A range of books and merchandise, including magazine holders and apparel, is also available, together with gift vouchers. The 'Customer Service' feature should answer any user queries.

GREAT FOR:
Australian magazines

magsonthenet.com

USA

LOWEST PRICES GUARANTEED
Mags on the Net offers more than 2000 magazine subscriptions up to a stated 95% off regular cover prices. Magazines from almost every genre are featured, including titles from 'Business & Finance', 'Fashion', 'Health & Fitness', 'Cooking' and 'Science & Nature'. You can also search for a specific title from an alphabetical list. There are collections of themed 'three packs' of specially chosen titles, including the 'Teen Pack', 'Bridal Pack' and 'Travel Pack'. An excellent FAQ section is also featured.

GREAT FOR:
All major titles

moviesunlimited.com — USA

THE MOVIE COLLECTOR'S WEBSITE
This Philadelphia-based company is one of the world's oldest video mail order companies. Recognised as one of the most comprehensive sources for hard-to-find titles, the store's catalogue features more than 800 pages of available titles at great prices. Search by movie title, actor or director, or from genres including 'Classics', 'Musicals', 'Foreign Films' and 'Television Shows'. You'll also find a range of movie-related books and posters.

GREAT FOR: Out-of-print video movies, classic movies

musicstack.com — USA

THE MUSIC MARKETPLACE
A clearing house for more than 3500 independent record stores, this e-store offers an amazing collection of rare vinyl records and out-of-print CDs. More than 19 million musical albums, vinyls and used CDs are featured, and you can search by artist, title, label or genre for a range of formats including CDs, vinyl, CD singles, CDRs and videos.

GREAT FOR: Rare music

opuscds.com

NZ

THE CLASSICAL MUSIC STORE
Specialising in classical music, Opus CDs features the best classical releases, together with MP3 samples, DVDs and related merchandise. Work your way through more than two dozen genres including baroque, chamber, easy listening and jazz, and read through Opus Notes on each album or listen to MP3 samples of individual tracks. A 'Review Section' includes excellent background information on releases and also some suggestions for similar titles. The site also has a comprehensive range of New Zealand music.

GREAT FOR:
Classical music

redhouse.co.uk

UK

THE HOME OF CHILDREN'S BOOKS
Redhouse is known as the 'home of children's books', offering the best titles for children from babies to teenagers, all at great value prices. Main categories include 'Favourites', 'Books for Babies', 'Books for 5-7 Years' and 'Teenage Fiction'. The site's top 10 books are also listed. Other features include the 'Classic Collection', the 'Reading Room' with an online reading group you can join, and 'Redhouse Reader Reviews', with new releases.

GREAT FOR:
Children's classics

rescuedbooks.com — USA

GENTLY USED HARD-COVERS

Specialising in gently used hardback library books, this e-store is the perfect place to locate out-of-print books or a childhood favourite that has been withdrawn from publication. Search the site for books by author or title, or from categories including 'Biographies', 'Fiction' and 'Non-Fiction'. You can also post your 'Book Wants' on the site in the event that the title is not currently in stock. A special Rescued Books 'Kids' section features hundreds of children's books including picture books, early readers and junior non-fiction titles. Gift certificates can also be purchased.

GREAT FOR:
Out-of-print books

secondspin.com — USA

DIRT CHEAP MUSIC

Online since 1996, Second Spin sells 'dirt cheap' used CDs, DVDs and games. Search by keyword, artist, album, title or director for a diverse range of titles. Latest arrivals are listed every 24 hours and you can also use the site to sell your old CDs, DVDs and games. Many out-of-production or hard-to-find titles are featured in the 'Collectibles' department. There are also regular 'Special Deals' and a 'Personal Favourites' feature, which allows you to keep track of stocked items by your favourite artist.

GREAT FOR:
CDs, DVDs

selectair.com.au

AUS

DELIVERY TO YOUR DOOR

Have the latest, coolest magazines from around the world delivered to your door by Selectair. Choose from 'Fashion', 'Design', 'Home' and 'Motoring' publications and enjoy free delivery. Current titles include UK *Vogue*, American *Elle*, *Country Life*, *World Interiors*, *Martha Stewart Living* and *FHM*. A full publication listing is alphabetically displayed in the 'Full Zine Listing' section.

GREAT FOR:
International magazines

simplyaudiobooks.com

USA

BEST-SELLERS ON TAPE

Selling exactly what its title suggests, this e-store boasts one of the best online audio book rental and sales services on the internet. With over 19,000 titles in 30 categories, chances are if it's not on this site it probably doesn't exist. Just like a regular bookstore, you'll find 'New Releases', together with 'Staff Picks', 'Oprah's Book Club List' and the '*New York Times* Best-sellers'. Genres include 'Business', 'Fiction', 'Children's' and 'Sci-Fi'. Catalogues can also be downloaded from the site.

GREAT FOR:
Best-sellers

the big names
INTERNATIONAL DEPARTMENT STORES

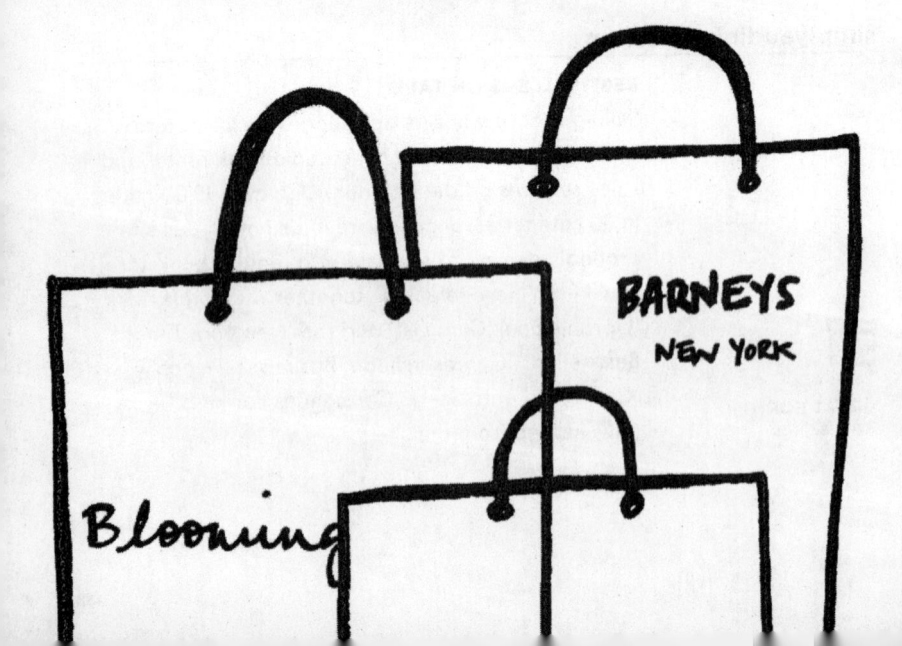

BARNEYS
NEW YORK

Blooming

ashford.com

USA

BIG NAMES, BIG DISCOUNTS

Browse through 10 departments, with promised savings of up to 60% off brand-name products at Ashford. More than 400 luxury brands are featured including Gucci, Burberry and Prada, with impressive product lines such as handbags, watches and fragrances. The site features a convenient cross-category keyword search and searches can be made by manufacturer name or product type. 'Ashford Outlet' provides further discounted items.

GREAT FOR:
Fragrances, jewellery, handbags

barneys.com

USA

FASHIONISTA HEADQUARTERS

You cannot leave your laptop without at least one visit to Barneys. A mecca for international fashionistas since 1923, Barneys stands for 'taste, luxury and humour'. Shop at their e-store for 'Women', 'Men', 'Home' and 'Baby'. Products include jewellery, handbags, fragrances, leather accessories, tableware and gifts. Look out for the exclusive range of Barneys handbags and totes available in a range of colours. The 'Barneys Co-op' department features slightly hipper, sharper and less expensive merchandise in all major product categories.

GREAT FOR:
Women's fashion, homewares

bergdorfgoodman.com USA

FIFTH AVENUE LANDMARK

Bergdorf Goodman (Bergdorfs to the locals) is a world famous luxury retailer. The store's website showcases the best of its wares with appearances by all the big names in fashion and design. Shop the 'Women's Collection', 'Shoes and Handbags', 'Jewellery' and 'Beauty' with the help of excellent product descriptions and photographs. Gift giving is made easy with luxurious gift suggestions for all the important people in your life. Keep an eye out for the 'BG Sale' for as much as 40% off selected merchandise.

GREAT FOR:
Women's fashion, men's gifts

bloomingdales.com USA

A BROWN BAG OF DESIGNER GOODIES

Established as a store in New York's lower east side by Joseph Bloomingdale in the 1860s, Bloomingdales is now an American shopping institution, with many locations. Thanks to this e-store you too can fill your 'little brown bag' with designer goodies. The women's range is a highlight and includes clothing, swimwear and intimate apparel. Browse throughout the 'Trends' section, which showcases major looks of the season. Current store catalogues can also be downloaded.

GREAT FOR:
Women's fashion, women's accessories, beauty products

colette.fr

FR

GREAT FOR:
Gifts, music

FRENCH SUPERSTORE
Style. Design. Art. Food. That's Colette, one of France's most famous and eclectic department stores, situated on the sophisticated Rue St Honoré in Paris. You'll find a modest selection of super stylish merchandise on this e-shop, with current items including the acclaimed Colette CD collections, toys by Trosselier and Claude Closky calendars. Download Colette's style magazine, *Le Colette*, from the site, and view a full store brand list. New products are added regularly.

fortunoff.com

USA

GREAT FOR:
Homewares, gifts

EVERYTHING FROM NECESSITIES TO NICETIES
A family-owned business since 1922, Fortunoff strives for 'excellence in quality, selection, value and service', offering all sorts of products including jewellery, tableware, home accessories, bedding and baby collections. Allow yourself plenty of time to search the site and, during the festive period, check out the famous 'Christmas Store' for assorted lights, ornaments and decorations.

harrods.co.uk
UK

NIP INTO KNIGHTSBRIDGE

The online store of this Knightsbridge institution offers a tempting collection of designer merchandise including women's apparel and accessories, men's essentials, children's wear, beauty collections, home décor items and the famous Harrods hampers. A range of 'Harrods Classic Collections' is also available, including the signature green shoppers, mugs, toiletries and souvenirs, all with the distinctive Harrods store branding. A 'Corporate Services' department is also available for corporate gift giving.

GREAT FOR:
Women's fashion, children's gifts

macys.com
USA

A RANGE LIKE NO OTHER

Perhaps equally well known for its annual Thanksgiving Parade as its great product range, the online Macy's store will not disappoint. Opening in 1858 in New York City, and growing to be one of America's largest department store retailers, Macy's is stocked full of products, including bedding, homewares, men and women's clothing and beauty collections. This e-store features an unbelievable volume of merchandise with all the major brands represented. Great clearance ranges can also be found in each product category.

GREAT FOR:
Women's fashion, men's fashion, homewares

marksandspencer.com
UK

AS BRITISH AS BIG BEN
With more than 400 stores across the United Kingdom today, Marks and Spencer began as a humble market stall in the late 1800s. This site offers online shopping for women's clothing, men's clothing, lingerie, children's wear, homewares and furnishings, all with a contemporary British feel. Head to the 'Site Map' for an excellent overview of the store's contents and features. Look out for the '3 for 2' deals exclusive to the store.

GREAT FOR:
Menswear, lingerie

neimanmarcus.com
USA

THE FINEST IN FASHION IS JUST THE BEGINNING
Renowned for its high-end merchandise, Neiman Marcus continues a tradition of distinguished retailing on this site. All the major departments are featured, including women and men's apparel, fashion accessories, beauty and homewares. Unlike many of its contemporaries, the store offers impeccable online assistance via an online chat feature. A 'Personal Shopper' service provides one-on-one sales service for all merchandise sold online.

GREAT FOR:
Women's fashion, accessories

nordstrom.com
USA

BURSTING WITH BRANDS
This Seattle-based retailer does the web thing well with this e-store. Shopping for women, men, children, beauty and the home is a breeze on the simply designed and easy-to-navigate site. Special shopping features include a gift-finder, an express checkout and the capacity for multiple shipping destinations. Seasonal catalogues are available online in a page-by-page format. Live online customer assistance is also available.

GREAT FOR:
Handbags, children's wear

overstock.com
USA

ONLINE OUTLET SHOPPING
At the risk of stating the obvious, this store is filled with manufacturers' overstocked product. You'll find everything from homewares, jewellery and sporting goods to electronics and apparel, all at a reported 40–80% off. All items are unused and warranties are offered on every purchase. Click on the 'New Stock' section for the newest stock arrivals.

GREAT FOR:
Homewares, electronics

petersofkensington.com.au — AUS

BOUTIQUE SYDNEY DEPARTMENT STORE

Peters of Kensington opened in 1977 and has become a Sydney shopping landmark. The store's website was launched in late 2000 and sells accessories, beauty items, cookware, homewares and more! Each department has its own 'Shopping Assistant' who can help you find what you're looking for by keyword, brand or price. Featured labels include Agent Provocateur, Bodum, Crabtree & Evelyn, Gucci, Krosno, Nigella Lawson and Swarovski. Check out the 'Christmas Shop' for Christmas cakes, decorations and gift baskets.

GREAT FOR: Homewares, travel goods

saksfifthavenue.com — USA

ONE OF THE BEST IN THE BUSINESS

The online presence of one of New York's most famous department stores is no less impressive than you would expect from one of the best retailers in the business. Launched in 2000, the site boasts merchandise for men, women and children. Shop by product or designer and trawl through the 'Sale' section for a comprehensive range of discounted items from most of the product categories. Current store catalogues are also able to be downloaded.

GREAT FOR: Women's fashion, accessories, men's fashion

walmart.com — USA

THE DISCOUNT DESTINATION

With a promise of across-the-board low prices, Walmart is the ultimate discount destination. The company's e-store is no exception, stocking an incredibly diverse product range. The site is divided into departments, including 'Electronics', 'Books', 'Jewellery' and 'Homewares', clearly labelled on blue tabs at the top of the page.

GREAT FOR:
Homewares, books

say it with style
SUPER STYLISH STATIONERY, CARDS & INVITATIONS

bellamuse.com　　　　　　　　　　　　　　　　　　　　　　　　　　USA

WHIMSICAL VINTAGE STATIONERY

Established in 2003 by artist and typographer Alicia Deck, this range of social stationery is sophisticated, yet whimsical. Drawing on a love of writing, humour and antique illustration, the current collection includes cards and stationery items, together with T-shirts for the whole family. Card designs include the cheeky 'She Drinks Like a Man' and 'My Sources Say Maybe' and can be purchased individually or in sets of six. The stationery range includes personalised greeting or note cards where any image from an extensive design library can be combined with your name or initials for a truly unique finish.

GREAT FOR: Special-occasion cards

birdinaskirt.com　　　　　　　　　　　　　　　　　　　　　　　　　　USA

ONE OF A KIND PAPER GOODS

No, this site does not offer a selection of wardrobe essentials for our feathered friends. Rather, Bird in a Skirt is a (self-described) purveyor of 'handmade goodies for humankind'. This e-store is a recent find of mine and, while it includes a range of bags, accessories and clothing, the paper goods range is definitely the highlight. The current selection includes blank cards, personalised note cards, and customised invitations and birth announcements. Flat card designs include animal silhouettes and a wood-grain apple. Custom-orders are welcome.

GREAT FOR: Handmade paper products

birksdean.com

AUS

CLASSIC PAPER PRODUCTS WITH A MODERN EDGE

This Melbourne-based team produce an outstanding collection of designer paper products including hand-bound photo books, journals and jotters. Current treats include the coffee-and-black tweed cloth jotters and the denim photo books. Embossing, in a range of font styles and sizes, is also available for most products. Payments cannot currently be made online – just print out the order form and phone/fax/mail your order request. The company is also a master in corporate gifts and presentation products including menus and diaries.

GREAT FOR:
Albums, notebooks

blissen.com

USA

FEW-OF-A-KIND PAPER GOODIES

Blissen is all about handcrafted limited-edition products. Their collection of cards and stationery currently includes the quirky 'Colour Your Own' Christmas cards and the stripy cheque book cosy. You can read all about the artist behind your chosen piece and new items are regularly added to the site. Because they are handmade, no two products will ever be exactly alike. Packages can be wrapped in cool gingham fabric pouches.

GREAT FOR:
Cards, stationery

boatmangeller.com — USA

FASHIONABLE PAPER COLLECTIONS

Searching for that perfect paper product? Then look no further than Boatman Geller. Combining the simplicity of stationery classics with a generous dash of freshness, the range features nine stationery collections in categories including 'Birth Announcements', 'Boxed Sets' and 'Gift Tags'. Design highlights include the 'Hamptons Collection' and the 'Toile Collection', based on the classic French design. Unlike many others, the gift tags on this site boast the same level of quality design and innovation as other pieces in the collections.

GREAT FOR:
Gift cards, correspondence cards

carrieskiddiecloset.com — USA

ALL-OCCASION STATIONERY & NOTE CARDS

Carries Kiddie Closet aims to provide the best quality personalised paper products for kids at the best possible prices. The collection includes more than 25 products including note cards, labels, candy bar wrappers, wedding cards and stickers. For serious playground kudos consider the personalised lunch-bag labels, which include a dinosaur and busy bee design. The 'Personalised Kids Chore Chart' can add a creative edge to even the most mundane household tasks. And forget pricey bribes, Carrie also has 'Potty Training Certificates' and 'Reward Kits'.

GREAT FOR:
Monogrammed cards

carrotandstickpress.com

USA

TRADITIONAL LETTERPRESS CARDS

Founded in 2000, Carrot & Stick Press provides an exceptional range of letterpressed paper products including folded cards, notebooks and place cards. Memorable designs include the mini red lobster and the chocolate argyle check. Customised designs are also available – take a look at 'Custom Portfolio' for past made-to-order pieces including hand-drawn maps and birth announcement cards. My most recent delivery included a beautifully presented full-colour catalogue.

GREAT FOR:
Cards for all occasions

celandinepaper.com

USA

CELEBRATING THE ART OF LUXURIOUS LETTERPRESS

The team at Celandine Paper celebrate the beauty and intimacy of written correspondence, tempting shoppers with a chic collection of letterpressed cards. Premium designs include the 'Letter Range' – white folded cards with a contrasting dark letterpressed letter of your choice. Birthday cards are available in sets of six – perfect for last minute card requirements – while baby announcement cards are letterpressed in two ink colours with personalised text.

GREAT FOR:
Birthday cards, thankyou cards

chelseapaper.com
USA

ALL STATIONERY FOR ALL OCCASIONS
Inspired by the cutting-edge style and sophistication of the Chelsea districts of London and New York, Chelsea Papers is one of the most comprehensive stockists of top-line stationery for all occasions. With over 40 brands available, products range from the latest hot pink or electric blue baby birth announcement cards (with not a bootie or bottle in site) through to the new stationery collection from uber bridal designer Vera Wang. An 'Etiquette' section on the site ensures that all invitation wording is phrase perfect.

GREAT FOR:
Baby cards, stationery, invitations

confoti.com
USA

ONE-OF-A-KIND CONFETTI
At Confoti your digital pictures are just a few steps away from being transformed into 3200 pieces of original confetti known as 'confoti'. This e-store promises to 'make every event unique, make every day memorable' with a range of personalised confoti and stickers. Great for weddings, birthdays and special occasions, the confoti is packaged in 60g bags with a mix of your photographs and colour accents, while the stickers are available in small (48 stickers) and large (96 stickers) sheets. Latest additions include the 'It's a Boy' range featuring blue shaded confetti with baby shots to celebrate the new arrival.

GREAT FOR:
Personalised confetti

debutanteriot.com

USA

UNEXPECTEDLY BEAUTIFUL CARDS & INVITATIONS

The brainchild of a former copywriter, Debutante Riot offers a fresh and modern range of cards, invitations and announcements. Browse through designs in categories including 'Bridal', ' Shower' and 'Party'. Forget naff Santas or saccharine angels, this holiday collection offers simple messages with a twist, including 'Have Yourself a Sparkling Little Christmas' opening up to the 'And a Really Peachy New Year' inside. For birth announcements with a difference, consider 'It's a Gentleman/Dude/Buckaroo' with an inner message introducing the new arrival. Note card sets are also available with appealingly cheeky messages.

GREAT FOR:
New arrival cards, holiday cards, note cards

dutchstationery.com

AUS

BEAUTIFULLY PRESENTED PERSONALISED CARDS & STATIONERY

Surprisingly, this site isn't Dutch. Rather, it's an e-boutique by two talented young Australians featuring a range of correspondence cards, personalised stationery, invitations and birth announcements. The products seamlessly blend the traditional with modern design. Correspondence cards are printed on subtly textured heavyweight card and have matching envelopes. For 'Birth Announcements' there's postcard-style cards with personalised photo-style stamps and the telegram-style card announcing your new arrival on a customised Telegram Office card.

GREAT FOR:
New arrival cards, birth announcements

firefly.bz

USA

STATIONERY FOR KIDS

Do kids these days send handwritten notes and letters? They will if the guys at FireFly have anything to do with it. Their designs are bursting with colour and freshness, ranging from a sassy giraffe to a more traditional candy-striped banner. The writing paper, note cards or gift tags are then personalised with your child's name. A choice of typefaces is also available for selection. The site also intends to add customised invitations to its range.

GREAT FOR:
Personalised note cards, creative stationery

frenchblueonline.com

USA

BECAUSE EVERY OCCASION DESERVES AN INVITATION

Founded in 2000 in Dallas (not France!), French Blue offers premium designed invitations, stationery and calling cards. As well as its own line, designs by Itty Bitty Inc, Paper Prince and Treehouse Designs are featured. Stocked product lines include special occasion invites, holiday cards and stationery for adults and children. The Holiday Photo Card is a particularly popular line – a personal photo is placed on a stylish card available in more than 30 colours and designs. Personalised text can also be included. Customised design preferences can also be accommodated.

GREAT FOR:
Customised invitations, stationery, stickers

guinevere.guink.com
USA

UNIQUE HAND-PAINTED DELIGHTS
Described as the place where modern sensibilities transform age-old crafts, this site specialises in letterpressed handpainted and hand-sewn cards and customised stationery. Featured characters include Harvey and Kimberley (a cat and a nearly hairless childhood doll, respectively), while stationery includes the handpainted range made from fine textured Italian paper. Look out for the 'Word Art' note cards with poetic sentiments on chocolate brown stitched cream paper with red letterpress text. A number of limited edition prints are also available.

GREAT FOR:
Cards, gift tags

hellolucky.com
USA

VINTAGE-INSPIRED PAPER WARE
Based in Berkeley, California, Hello Lucky is a boutique letterpress print and design studio. The collection incorporates note cards, invitations and related social stationery pieces – all printed on high-quality cream card stock with matching envelopes. Design categories include 'Baby', 'Thankyou', 'Everyday' and 'Party Invites'. Gift wrap and customised baby books are new additions to the site.

GREAT FOR:
Stationery, thankyou cards, get well cards

iomoi.com   USA

E-STATIONERY PIONEERS

Iomoi is a stationery site like no other. Together with traditional stationery items, Iomoi sells 'e-stationery' – a selection of online stationery enabling users to send emails on stylishly designed 'e-letterhead'. This irresistible union of cutting-edge technology and traditional design is truly impressive. A selection of 'off-line' stationery items is also available, including writing papers, note cards and address labels featuring simple yet exquisite images in a variety of colours. Designs range from classic to cool and include mini two-tone totes together with the silhouette of the perfect Tod's-style driving loafer.

GREAT FOR:
e-letterhead, all-occasion note cards

jellyandanchovy.com   USA

SCRUMPTIOUS HANDMADE STATIONERY

For 'real scrumptious handmade stationery' log onto Jelly and Anchovy. Paying clear homage to the 1950s, the handcrafted cards and social stationery items include the multiple choice range and some snappy couture clutches. Each piece is distinctly original and not made until you order it. All paper goods are packaged in sparkly clear boxes, kraft paper boxes or cellophane sleeves. Customised ribbon note cards are new additions to the collection.

GREAT FOR:
Everyday note cards

katespaperie.com

USA

AMERICA'S PREMIER PAPER GOODS STORE

This site offers an unmatched range of papers (more than 4000 styles), cards, albums, journals, calendars and writing instruments. Despite the extensive product range, the site is surprisingly easy to use and, as well as standard categories, it also separates ranges into distinct 'Collections', together with gift ideas. The signature 'Kate's Collection', in particular, features a stunning selection of cards and writing papers in fresh, bright hues. The store's current catalogue can also be downloaded online. Oh, and yes there actually is a Kate!

GREAT FOR:
Cards, stationery, ribbons, gifts

kikki-k.com.au

AUS

SWEDISH HOME/OFFICE STYLE

Swedish design meets Australian sensibility at Kikki K. The brainchild of self-confessed stationery addict Kristina Karlson, the site features a unique range of inspiring home/office stationery and accessories. Product picks include coordinated notebooks, lever arch folders, paper and storage boxes up to A3 size. From natural kraft, to soothing olive and a classic gloss white, all décor styles are accommodated. Starter home/office collections (in 8- or 13-piece sets) provide excellent value for money. The site also provides some practical tips for those taking the working-from-home route.

GREAT FOR:
Storage boxes, notebooks, folders

kolo.com
USA

A PASSION FOR PHOTOGRAPHIC PRESENTATION

Learn. Shop. Create. Those are the clear instructions from the team at Kolo, a company committed to creating an unmatched range of photo albums and accessories destined to become future heirlooms. All albums are archival quality, acid free and available with leather, cloth or paper coverings. Gift products are also available, including the 'mini-mini' – an assorted palette of eight mini-albums made from Italian paper with an accented ribbon tie. The 'Havana' photo boxes are also worth exploring. Made from archival board, European cloth or leather, the boxes are inspired by the iconic Cuban cigar box.

GREAT FOR:
Photo albums, photo storage boxes

lovelydesign.com
USA

HANDCRAFTED PAPER GOODS

I have only recently found Lovely Design, and immediately fell in love with this range of handmade items including hand-bound notebooks and beautiful journey books hand-stitched with wax-lined thread. I recently purchased the 'I Miss You Mail Set', a stationery set created from 100% recycled vintage maps and papers. A must-stop for one-of-a-kind gifts or unique additions to your own stationery drawer.

GREAT FOR:
Notebooks, note cards

luxepaperie.com

USA

SEND SOMETHING CHIC

A boutique stationery store, Luxe Paperie promises 'stylish stationery for every person on your list'. With a passion for unique and special paper products, the site specialises in letterpress stationery, together with gift cards, invitations, boxed notes and gift wrap. Featured brands include Snow & Graham, Lunalux, Little Tree Press, and Two Piglets, many of which are not readily available in Australia. Shop by 'Brand', 'Occasion' or 'Type' and take a look at the chic range of boxed note card sets.

GREAT FOR:
Greeting cards, invitations, gift wrap

---

mjtrim.com

USA

A CANDY STORE FOR CREATIVE PEOPLE

I found out about this brand of premium trims in a recent edition of a Martha Stewart magazine. Described as a 'candy store for creative people', M&J Trimming stocks an incredible range of trims including ribbons, beads and feathers. Of particular interest is the 'Ribbon Centre', which features more than a dozen ribbon types including grosgrain, organza and silk. The striped ribbon collection alone is available in more than 25 colour combinations. Take a look on the opening page for instructions on how to tie the perfect bow.

GREAT FOR:
Grosgrain ribbons

paper-girl.com
USA

CREATIVE CUSTOMISED INVITATIONS
Bored with ecru and white paper with a black cursive type, Paper-Girl vowed to create something fresh, new and different for her special day. The ultimate result was the sexy social stationery range on this site. For wedding invites think luxurious cards slipped into a faux mink pocket, for the baby shower its an invite packaged as a cloth nappy, while for chic correspondence look no further than the unique writing papers featuring luxe fabric and appliqués sewn onto Fabriano paper.

GREAT FOR:
Invitations

paperieandco.com
USA

CELEBRATE IN STYLE
From the candy-striped colour palette to the whitest of white smiles, this site screams, if not bellows, southern hospitality. Based in Dallas, Texas, Paperie & Co offers an outstanding selection of invitations, stationery, cards, gift wrap, journals, albums and more. The site is clearly separated into 'For Weddings', 'For Babies' and 'For Holidays', allowing you to easily satisfy your specific social stationery needs. One of the more unusual products is photofetti – confetti made from your snapshots and combined with colourful accents. The site map provides a comprehensive, if slightly overwhelming, listing of specific product lines.

GREAT FOR:
Invitations,
stationery,
journals

paperprincess.com USA

ONE-STOP SHOP FOR SOCIAL STATIONERY

Every girl wants to be a princess (minus the relentless media attention and inevitable mistress in the wings), don't they? Well, if a regal appointment is not on your horizons, then at least your paper can have the princess touch. With a vibrant collection of cards, invitations and stationery, Paper Princess stocks a premium collection of paper products. The personalised post-it notes make a creative addition to any stationery collection.

GREAT FOR:
Holiday cards, stationery, office accessories

paperstyle.com USA

CARDS & STATIONERY — BIG & SMALL

With offerings from over 200 manufacturers and a total of more than 8000 items available, Paper Style is one of the internet's most comprehensive stationery sites. Whilst not as slickly designed as some more boutique-style e-retailers, the site is easy to navigate, despite the extensive product range. Everything from traditional wedding invitations to funky embossed calling cards is available. The site also includes a helpful selection of suggested wording for all occasions.

GREAT FOR:
Invitations, cards, scrapbooking supplies

pinklovesbrown.com

USA

LOVINGLY HANDMADE PAPER GOODIES

Featuring the artwork of Nicole Balch, a self-described master face painter, window dresser and dinosaur muralist, this site offers a small yet charming range of handmade cards, invitations and stationery. Designs include the 'Craft Collection' featuring sewing items such as a needle and thread silk-screened onto cream card. Occasion-specific cards, including birthdays, thankyous and weddings, combine with personalised stationery to create a unique selection of traditional paper products with a modern twist. A custom invitation service is available.

GREAT FOR:
Birthday cards, thankyou cards, bookplates

ragandbone.com

USA

EXQUISITE, HANDCRAFTED BOOKS

Rag and Bone is a bindery boutique that creates hand-bound paper products. Product themes include 'Baby', 'Wedding' and 'Everyday' and include photo albums, books, binders and journals. Baby's First Book is a best-seller containing 24 whimsically designed pages and a vellum envelope for special treasures. The blank-page journals are equally impressive and, with heavy-weight paper, can accommodate pen or pencil entries. The new 'Digital Photo Album' provides a fun way to show off your digital snaps, with pages suitable for ink jet printing. Cover options for most products include brights, neutrals or patterned silk fabrics.

GREAT FOR:
Photo albums, photo binders, journals

r-nichols.com USA

NOTE CARDS WITH CHARM

This is truly handmade stationery – the main shot on the site actually shows Mr Nichols himself, scissors in hand, cutting a design for one of his super sexy cards. The collections include 'Baby', 'Beauty', 'NYC' and 'Riviera' designs printed on the finest quality cream-coloured card. New designs are introduced twice a year, although some classic styles remain. A T-shirt range has recently been introduced. The site also includes some witty words from the paper prince himself in the 'Ross Nichols Says' section.

GREAT FOR:
All-occasion cards

seejanework.com USA

THE DESTINATION FOR OFFICE STYLE

See Jane Work is the self-described 'destination of office style and organisation'. Look out for designer binders, desktop accessories, labels, totes and waste-paper baskets in styles and designs ranging from beach-side chic to corporate conservative. Turning the potentially drab into fab, take a look at the patterned elastic bands and contemporary chrome stapler. 'Pulling it Together' provides some clever gift suggestions and tips for better office organisation.

GREAT FOR:
Journals, note cards, storage items

smythson.co.uk — UK

TRADITIONAL BRITISH STATIONER

Smythson of Bond Street is a London retailing institution. As well as premium leather goods, the brand is renowned for its exquisite stationery range including personalised writing papers, motif cards, gift enclosures and pens. Packaged in sets of 100, the name-engraved correspondence cards are legendary and available in three sizes. For note cards with a less traditional feel, look at the gold-and-black handbag motif available in sets of 10 cards with tissue-lined envelopes. All stationery items are packaged in the signature blue Smythson box.

GREAT FOR: Personalised stationery, leathergoods

stranodesigns.com — USA

BOUTIQUE-STYLE GROSGRAIN RIBBONS

Any good gift giver knows that the wrapping is almost as important as the gift itself, and for those in search of the perfect ribbon, look no further than Strano Designs. This site offers an impressive collection of hard-to-find boutique striped grosgrain ribbons for purchase by the metre or roll. Ribbons are separated into widths (from approximately 9mm to 50mm) and design styles, including 'Staci's Stitched' and 'Riva's Dots'. Current highlights include 'Dottie's Pink', a fuchsia ribbon with electric blue and lime dots, and the 'Neapolitan', a stunning blend of pink, white and chocolate stripes.

GREAT FOR: Striped ribbons, stitched ribbons

sugarbeanpress.com USA

RETRO-INSPIRED HANDMADE CARDS

Email, schmemail say the girls at Sugar Bean Press. Effortlessly combining the traditional art of letterpress with sophisticated design, this company produces a range of witty cards and other stationery items, including the 'Cosmopolitan' range featuring retro fashion prints in striking aqua and olive green. And, as the girls attest, whilst saying thank you is good, sending a thankyou is even better (check out the 'World Traveller' thankyou set for a note of appreciation with a difference). Minimum online order of US$20.

GREAT FOR:
note cards, thankyou cards, invitations

sugarpaper.com USA

CUSTOM-DESIGNED LETTERPRESS STATIONERY

This is one of those sites you just know you're going to like. With a simple yet stylish design, Sugar Paper has a select range of paper products, namely traditional letterpress stationery, together with flat-printed note cards and boxed card sets. The letterpress products in particular are very impressive – I still receive complements every time I send one of my rich cream note cards with fuchsia pink pressed initials. A custom design service is also available.

GREAT FOR:
Stationery, cards

tigerandjones.com USA

DISTINCTIVE YET CLASSIC INVITATIONS

Sure emails are convenient, but they're not handcrafted, distinctive or luxurious, unlike the delectable collection of stationery, invitations and cards by Tiger & Jones. Distinctly separated into four categories: 'Imprintable', '18K Keepsakes', 'Personal Stationery' and 'Weddings', the products are manufactured with traditional methods including letterpress printing, hand-stitching and hand-dyed ribbons. For a truly unique purchase, take a look at the '18K Keepsakes' – single cards with 18K double-plated charms with wording like 'I am Smitten with Love' and 'Thinking of You'.

GREAT FOR:
Invitations, cards

traylorpapers.com USA

INNOVATIVE INVITES

Whether you want to celebrate, commiserate or congratulate, this site has a card for you. With over 40 featured brands, including Quick Click Chic and Jack and Lulu (my favourite), Traylor Papers is your one-stop paper products shop. The range of personalised note cards is especially impressive and can be teamed with coordinating stamps and stickers.

GREAT FOR:
Invitations, stationery, note cards

wrapsody.com

UK

GREAT FOR:
Personalised wrapping paper

CREATE YOUR OWN GIFT WRAP

Wow! You can actually create your own wrapping paper! I stumbled across this site by accident and just had to try it out. The results were impressive, and seeing my family snapshots on wrapping paper certainly provided a very personal touch to the gift-giving process. Photographs, drawings and even text can be featured, and a standard order includes two sheets of gift wrap. Paper is sent in a secure postal tube.

something different
THE WEIRD & WONDERFUL GOES ONLINE

aboutthedress.com USA

REMEMBERING THE GOWN

Sure there's the bride, the groom, the ring, the bridal party and the cake, but let's face it, when it comes to weddings it's all about the dress. Fashion illustrator Jennifer Angilello knows this and offers a remarkable service – she creates what she describes as an 'elegant illustration of your wedding gown'. Send off your photographs and dress details and she will create a stylized 11 x 14 inch illustration in an antiqued silver or gold frame. A unique way to remember what you wore on your special day, and no moth balls required!

GREAT FOR:
Individual artwork

airsicknessbags.com USA

A TRIBUTE TO AIRCRAFT HAPPY SACKS

According to this site, 'airsickness bags are art'. Whilst this claim may be entirely subjective, you'll have loads of laughs browsing through this cyber museum featuring dozens of airsickness bags (or Happy Sacks as pilots apparently call them) from all the major airlines including Qantas, Singapore Airlines, Virgin, British Airways and Air France. Visit the online gift shop for airsickness bag posters and, for those who feel themselves succumbing to the unbridled excitement of airsickness bag collecting, a free starter kit (consisting of three bags) is also available. My only question now is, with the rise of digital photography, do the bags still double as send away photo developing envelopes?

GREAT FOR:
International airsickness bags

dogue.com.au

AUS

CANINE COUTURE

According to this e-store, fashion hounds can't stop barking about Dogue, the house of canine couture. Started in the late 1990s, the store features a super stylish dogalogue of designer canine carry bags, outfits, collars, jewellery and accessories for your pampered pooch. Browse through classic four-poster canopy beds, Yves Saint Bernard carry cases, denim coats and handpainted feeding bowls, all certain to please even the most design-savvy pup. Seasonally reduced items are clearly listed in the 'Specials' department, and you can even sign up for dog birthday registration. Gift certificates are also available.

GREAT FOR: Clothing, accessories & gifts for dogs

elifesize.com

USA

CARDBOARD CELEBRITIES

Fancy the latest Hollywood starlet or revered statesman attending your next soirée? Well, forget about dealing with pesky publicists or negotiating big bucks for personal appearances and simply visit Elifesize. You'll find life-size cardboard cut-outs and stand-ups of all of your favourite celebs including Abbott and Costello, George Bush, Jennifer Aniston, Paris Hilton and the newly introduced 'true to size' Jesus. You can search by celebrity name or from categories including 'Cartoons', 'Hollywood Legends', Politics', 'Sport' and 'Television'. You can even have your own custom cardboard stand-up made from your personal photograph.

GREAT FOR: Life-size celebrity stand-ups

fingermagic.com

USA

ORIGAMI GOES ONLINE

This site is the result of one woman's obsession with the 'magical' art of origami. In order to share her passion, Cindy Ng created Finger Magic, featuring a range of incredible origami kits including 'Bunny Origami', 'Froggie Origami' and 'Turtle Origami'. Each kit contains 20 sheets of pre-printed paper complete with step-by-step photographic instructions. Origami card-making kits are also available, including 'Origami Mini Skirts', 'Origami Tulips' and 'Origami High Heel'. Origami gift boxes are also stocked, together with origami earrings packaged in mini origami gift boxes.

GREAT FOR:
Origami kits

illinoisretail.com/humor/bobs

USA

CHOKING HAZARDS GUARANTEED

Actually titled 'One Eyed Bob's Inappropriate Toys for Children', this site is a toy store with a definite dark side. Refusing to bow to any form of political correctness, Bob proudly displays a controversial collection of toys and games including the Human Cloning Kit, Road Kill Bingo, and Serial Killer Trading Cards. There are also hours of creative play to be found in the Alien Abductee Adventure set or, for the budding surgeon, the Child's Plastic Surgery Kit. Thank God for Bob.

GREAT FOR:
Unusual toys for twisted tots

Iloveyoumorethanchocolate.com
UK

DECORATIVE CHOCOLATE SQUARES

A phrase many of us have often been tempted to use, I Love You More Than Chocolate is an e-store dedicated to exquisite individually handmade chocolate squares featuring a range of creative designs. Consider 'Decorative' chocolates with a coffee cup on a pink blush chocolate square; 'Black & White' designs including chocolate noughts and crosses; or 'Funky' for a stiletto, handbag and lipstick trio on white chocolate. There are also squares featuring Happy Birthday! or Stressed? messages. Miniature and seasonal ranges complete the collection.

GREAT FOR:
Handmade chocolate treats

lawnmowerworld.co.uk
UK

MOWING MEMORABILIA

This site is dedicated to the often neglected yet fascinating world of the humble lawnmower. As well as taking a peek at the lawnmowers of the rich and famous (including the treasured grass-cutters of the Prince of Wales and Queen's Brian May), this online museum also features the museum shop where you'll find lawnmower design pens, mugs, cards and posters. The store also offers an authentic replica of a Sharks 100-year-old mower, which sounds terribly impressive. Oh, and don't forget to look out for the newly launched DVD 'Lawnmowerworld' promising a glimpse into the fascinating history of garden machinery.

GREAT FOR:
Mowing souvenirs

letterlover.net

USA

WHEN ONLY THE RIGHT WORDS WILL DO

Ever wanted to write a witty/sensitive/utterly impressive letter but just couldn't find the right words? If so, then this site can help. You see, Letter Lover provides individual letters for any occasion or situation – love letters, apologies, break-ups and more. You can read through some sample letters written by an English and Journalism graduate whose hates include letters left undelivered and things left unsaid. All you need to do is provide some details of your situation, then just sit back and await receipt of a letter you literally couldn't have written better yourself.

GREAT FOR:
Letters to impress

minimus.biz

USA

GOOD THINGS IN SMALL PACKAGES

Credit-card-sized phones, pencil-thin laptops, pint-sized smart cars. Is it just me, or is everything getting smaller these days? They certainly are at this e-store – a purveyor of miniature-sized food, personal care and pharmacy items. You'll find everything from cereals, condiments, dips, jams and syrups to shampoos, skincare and sun protection, often packaged at a quarter of their usual size. Great for travelling or just because the packaging is so adorable! The store also stocks a line of pre-made mini-kits including the 'Cold & Flu Care Package', the 'Car Essentials Kit' and 'Breakfast on the Go'. Head to the 'Site List' for a full alphabetical listing of all stocked products.

GREAT FOR:
Mini food products

mobi-usa.com
USA

DESIGNER LUNCH BAGS
In case you didn't know it, plain plastic lunch bags are so yesterday. Today's leading school lunches are proudly displayed in designer-style zipper bags by Mobi Inc. Featuring bold stripes, bright floral patterns, yellow smiley faces and the signature seal logo, there are 20 bags in each box, with each bag measuring 16.7cm x 13.25cm. Thanks to this store, now even the blandest cheese sandwich and green apple combo can look positively cool.

GREAT FOR:
Creative zip-lock bags

netjets.com
USA

EVEN BETTER THAN FIRST CLASS
Searching for a gift for that special person who has everything, well how about a private jet? Actually its fractional jet ownership, which basically gives the recipient all the benefits of whole aircraft ownership but at a promised 'fraction' of the cost. You can even buy a 'Marquis Jet Card' – a single-year, 25-hour pre-paid lease of flight time starting at US$115,900. For the more frequent flyer there are fractional shares from US$406,250 for approximately 50 hours of annual flying time on a choice of 14 aircraft types. Possibly not the most practical purchase, but a girl can dream.

GREAT FOR:
Travelling in style

polka.com.au — AUS

COUTURE CAKES & COOKIES

Established in 2003 by a talented pastry chef, Polka Dot offers a delicious range of original cookies and cakes decorated with a unique style. For weddings you'll find stunning creations including the Queen of Sheba chocolate torte and a lemon, lavender and buttercream cake, as well as cookies in orchid and pear designs. There's also a stunning birthday cookie range and original birthday cakes featuring fresh and edible decorations. Seasonal ranges, including Christmas and Easter cookies, are also available. The store provides customised cookies for corporate promotions and events.

GREAT FOR: Designer cookies

schoolfolio.com — USA

HOLD-ALLS FOR JUNIOR ART

Sure we all love kids' artwork – the finger-painted self portraits, the abstract sketches of an unidentifiable animal and fifth-grade projects are priceless. But where to store these treasured mementos? This e-store has the answer and it's school folios. The folios come in two styles – the 'All in One' folio with six inner folders and pre-printed labels, and the latest model, the 'Single Folio', a more portable version available in four colourful designs. The company's message is to 'Save the Art', and to that end a percentage of profits goes to American schools or School Folio's non-profit organisation committed to youth art projects.

GREAT FOR: Art folios

shop2.mms.com — USA

PERSONALISED CANDY

There's only one thing better than a bowl of rich chocolate m & ms and that's a bowl of personalised m & ms. This site allows you to customise one side of the m & ms with your own word or message. There are 21 colours available, and you can opt for a single colour batch or a blended mix. You can also purchase a range of m & ms merchandise including T-shirts, dispensers, cookie jars and snow globes.

GREAT FOR:
Original m & ms

specialeffectscookbook.com — USA

THE MOST EXCITING PARTY FOOD EVER

This e-store sells the acclaimed *Special Effects Cookbook*, filled with safe and easy recipes for food that moves, erupts, snaps, glows and pops! The book features more than 100 incredibly edible movie-type special effects recipes using ordinary food ingredients. Stand-outs include the 'Beating Heart Cake', which pulsates just like a real heart, and the edible erupting chocolate volcano cake with strawberry flavoured lava. There's also the world's only 'Eat Yer Face' jelly moulds, a creative way to make an exact jelly replica of your face.

GREAT FOR:
Explosive recipes

subversivecrossstitch.com — USA

CRAFT WITH ISSUES

There are many ways to deal with unresolved anger – physical violence, legal action, high-pitched tirades, the list goes on. But next time your temper is frayed, why not direct your attitude into something a little more craft-oriented. Like, say, cross stitch. The team at Subversive Cross Stitch have a unique selection of kits including 'Bite Me', 'Life Sucks Then You Die', 'Get Lost' and 'Babies Suck'. Basic and Deluxe kits are available and include patterns, cross-stitch fabric and embroidery thread. New styles are regularly added.

GREAT FOR: Unique cross stitch kits

thebirthdaysock.com — USA

ANOTHER SPECIAL STOCKING TO HANG

No matter what your age, birthdays are a special day. In 2001, Summer Robertson was searching for a way to get more presents. Her answer was to hang up an old brown sock in the hope that it would be filled with goodies on her birthday morning. It worked for Christmas, why not for birthdays? Fast forward, and Summer now produces a range of birthday socks available in a range of colours including blue, yellow, green and purple. Made of 100% nylon the socks are extra long to fit presents of all shapes and sizes.

GREAT FOR: Unique gift socks

treatsfromhome.com.au — AUS

FOOD-FILLED LIFELINE FOR BRITISH EXPATS

Dreaming of Marmite? Craving Walkers salted crisps? Ready to kill for some Sherbet Lemons? If you're a Brit living in Australia, chances are you're missing your favourite sweets, crisps and gourmet delicacies from home. Treats from Home comes to the rescue with a selection of British chocolate bars, sweets, crisps, biscuits and soft drinks. A collection of hampers is also available including the 'Tea & Bikkie' hamper, the 'Sweet Shop' hamper and the 'Breakfast Basket' hamper. You can also make your own hamper choosing individual items from the listed product categories.

GREAT FOR: British chocolates, crisps & gourmet goodies

uncommongoods.com — USA

CREATIVE GIFTS & HOME ACCESSORIES

For those looking for products outside the usual (gift) box, take a look at Uncommon Goods, an online store with a commitment to providing creatively designed merchandise at affordable prices. The store promises 'anything but ordinary' products in a range of departments including 'Dining', 'Paper', 'Jewellery' and 'Home Accents'. A number of special features add to the appeal of the store, including profiles of artists and designers, the highlighting of handmade goods, and the 'Better to Give' program enabling a portion of your order to be donated to your choice of non-profit organisation.

GREAT FOR: Gifts with a twist

Security and shipping
EVERYTHING YOU NEED TO KNOW

ONLINE SECURITY

For many would-be internet shoppers, online security is an issue of major concern. We've all heard those horror stories of newbie shoppers finding themselves the innocent victims of credit card fraud once their details are released into cyberspace.

However, in my experience of online shopping over the past five years, I am yet to have a negative shopping experience. This is, I'm sure, partly due to a bit of luck, but more importantly I have adopted the following principles when considering whether to purchase from a specific site.

- Shop on secure websites. A secure website should be clearly marked by way of a padlock or similar symbol, or by specific wording to the effect that the site uses a secure server. There may also be an 's' after the 'http' in the web page address. This means that your information is encrypted for transmission over the internet, minimising the risk of internet fraud.

- Use a single credit card when making your online purchases – this will make it easy to keep a record of your purchases and also identify any suspicious transactions.

- Read through the privacy and security policies of individual sites. You should always aim to keep your private information private. Obviously you need to provide certain details to enable a transaction to be processed, but beware of providing additional personal information as many sites may then on-sell such information to third parties. This should be detailed in the privacy and security sections of the site.

- Always print out copies of your orders/receipts and keep them (at least) until your goods have been received.

- Trust your instincts. As with a bricks-and-mortar store, if something about an e-store makes you feel uncomfortable or wary, shop elsewhere. Similarly, if something seems too good to be true, chances are, it probably is.

It is also important to remember that, on the whole, online shopping is just as safe, if not safer, than traditional offline shopping. Much of the common sense you adopt when doing your regular shopping also applies online.

INTERNATIONAL MAIL FORWARDING

Many international shopping sites, including many of those listed in this book, do not provide shipping to Australia. Many will only ship to the USA and in my early online shopping days I thought that meant I couldn't make any purchases from these stores. That was, until I discovered the joy of international mail forwarding. Completely legal, essentially it is a service whereby you pay for a US-based street address to which your chosen mail can be sent. You then use this address for all your online ordering where a US address is required. Your packages are then forwarded to your regular Australian mail address.

There are a number of companies providing this service and you usually pay an initial set-up fee, then shipping fees for individual items. For several years I have been with a company called myus.com. I have a US address that I provide to e-retailers who forward any purchased items to my address at the myus.com offices. When a package arrives I receive an advisory email from myus.com and then have the choice of having any packages sent immediately or waiting until the middle of the month when all my held items are usually forwarded to me.

A good starting point when considering which international mail-forwarding service would best suit your needs is a site called www.mail-forwarding advisor.com. It provides comparative information on some of the major providers.

Each provider has pros and cons depending on a number of issues, including:

* how often you expect to have mail delivered to your US address,
* whether you expect to have only documents delivered, or larger packages as well,
* how quickly you wish to be able to receive any items, and
* whether you can have multiple users for your account.

In the rare event that an Australian credit card cannot be used on a specific site, many of these providers also offer a 'Personal Shopping' service, whereby for a small fee they can make purchases for you and arrange shipping to Australia.

Regardless of which provider you choose, an international mail-forwarding account is a must for any serious net shopper. In addition to receiving goods you could not have otherwise purchased, you can also receive store catalogues and special mail offers not usually available to Australian shoppers.

PAYPAL

In exploring the global shopping mall, you may well come across a payment means called Paypal. Many sites, American ones in particular, use this system to securely process all online payments. A global leader in safe online payments, Paypal allows you to provide your credit card details, with future payments then processed via Paypal and not individual merchants. This means you are only providing your information to one party and they are the ones who make the payment to individual web retailers. Signing up for Paypal is free and you can also use it for ebay transactions. If you are considering any international shopping, I would highly recommend you visit the Paypal site (www.paypal.com) and consider opening an account.

CUSTOMS & DUTIES

For imported goods purchased online, it is important to establish whether sales tax or duties will be payable. The website will usually address this issue in the 'Shipping' section of their site, but in most cases it is the responsibility of the purchaser to pay import duties, if any, payable once goods reach Australia. If you are unsure whether any taxes will be payable, check on the government's website at www.customs.gov.au. It is also important to note that there are many cases (e.g. with gifts) where duty or taxes are not payable.

INDEX

A
Agnès B 69
airsickness bags 167
albums 147, 160
Anya Hindmarch 69
aromatherapy 49, 66, 102
   see also *body-care* and *fragrances*
artwork 104, 112, 114, 165, 167-169
   folios 173

B
babies
   accessories 7-24, 42
   bags 8, 12, 16, 22, 72
   bedding (including blankets) 8, 12-25, 32, 102, 104, 109-110
   books 8, 133
   clothes 6-25, 31, 137
   costumes 14
   décor items 6-8, 17-19, 21, 23, 25-26, 32
   furniture 8, 10, 13, 18, 26
   gift boxes 11
   music 21
   organic products 20
   stationery 12, 150-151
   toys 6-26
bathing products see *body-care*
bathrobes 49, 70
bathroom see *homewares* and *towels*
beanbags 28, 103, 110
beauty 47-67, 72, 123, 138
   see also *make-up*, *body-care*, *skincare* and *hair-care*
bedding 102, 104-105, 108-111, 114, 116, 118-119
   cashmere 104
   handcrafted 6
   handknitted 12
   organic 102
   see also *babies* and *children*
Beth Bowley 80
Better To Give program 176
Blablabla 8
Blaec 70
body-care
   men's 97
   women's 48-53, 56-66
bookcases 107
bookplates 160
books 121-125, 144
   architecture 122
   audio books 124-125, 135
   biographies 121, 124
   business 123
   children's 8, 42, 44, 123, 133-134
   cookbooks 127, 174
   download 125
   new releases 123
   non-fiction 122
   out-of-print 134
   rare books 121, 124
bridal wear 73
briefcases 91
Burberry 137

C
cakes 173
Calvin Klein 73, 96
candles 49, 66-67, 102-103
cards 146-164,
CDs 121, 126, 128-9, 134, 139
   see also *music*
celebrity stand-ups 168
Celine 71
Chantal Thomas 88
children 28-46, 105, 142-143
   accessories 28-33, 44
   audio books 125
   beanbags 28, 110
   bedding 28-29, 32-34, 39-46, 118
   body-care 42
   books 42, 44, 123, 133-134
   car seats 46
   clothing 2, 28-44, 69, 76
   décor items 28-29, 32-34, 40-46

181

furniture 43, 36-37, 41
games 31, 35-36, 38, 41, 45-46
hair-care 37
lunch bags 172
movies 126
music 121
musical instruments 32
sleepwear 30, 39, 118
stationery 152
strollers 46
towels 28, 40, 43
toys 31-46
train sets 45
chocolate 170, 176
christenings 32
christmas 139, 143, 173
 cards 147, 151
Citizens of Humanity 82
clothes see *babies*, *children*, *women's fashion* and *men's fashion*
coaster sets 115
confetti 150, 158
corporate gifts 100, 140
craftwork kits 175
credit cards 177
crystal 115
currency issues 3
currency conversion 3
cushions 106-109, 112-113
customs and duties 179

D
décor items 101-119, 176
 see also *babies* and *children*
decorating ideas 105, 107, 111
Diane von Furstenberg 83
Diesel 71, 83
dogs 168
DVDs 123 see also *music*
 storage 117

E
electronics 100, 142, 144
 games 129
embroidery kits 175
Emilio Pucci 82

F
Facial care see *skincare*
Fendi 72
film see *movies*
Flavio Olivera 80
Flora and Henri 21
food 171, 173-174, 176
fragrances 48-49, 52, 55-58, 60-67, 72, 137
 home 52, 55, 58, 116, 118
 men's 56
French Connection 96
furniture 102, 105, 107-108, 110, 112-113, 119
 children's 8, 10, 13, 18, 26

G
Gap 74
garden 102, 114
gift socks 175
glasswear 106
 see also *homewares*
Gucci 137, 143
gumboots 89

H
Hair-care
women's 51-53, 59, 62-63, 66
handbags 69, 71-82, 137, 142
home office 117
home organisation 110, 113
homeopathic products 52
homewares 76, 88, 101-119, 123, 137, 139-144, 176

I
international mail forwarding 178
invitations 146, 150-153, 157-159, 162-164
iPod bags 80

J
jewellery 79-80, 81, 111, 137, 144, 176
Juicy Couture 83

K
Kate's Collection 155
kitchenware see *homewares*

L

La Perla 72
Laptop totes 81
laundry accessories 86, 112, 116
lawnmower memorabilia 170
letter-writing 171
lighting 103, 105, 107-108, 110-111, 113-114, 118
lingerie see *women's fashion*
lip balms 51, 59
lollies 174
Louis Vuitton 72
Lotta 70
luggage 61, 66, 76-79, 83, 90

M

make-up 48-49, 54, 56, 57, 60-67
magazines 127, 130-131, 135
m&ms 174
mail forwarding 178
massage products 53
   see also *body-care*
maternity wear 71, 73, 85
Marc Jacobs 71, 82
men's fashion
   accessories 91-100
   apparel 6, 22, 69, 72, 75, 90-100, 140-143
   body-care 92, 95, 97
   custom-design 94
   fragrances 56
   gifts 94-96, 100
   skincare 92, 97
   sleepwear 94, 94, 100
Michael Kors 88
miniature items 171
monogram service, men's 95
Moschino 7
movies 126
   out-of-print videos 132
music
   CDs 121, 126, 128-129, 134, 139
   children's 21
   classical 133
   DJ equipment 129
   DVDs 121, 129, 134
   rare 128, 132
   videos 121
   vinyl 129

N

Nigella Lawson 143
notebooks and journals 147, 149, 155-156, 158, 160-161

O

office products 100, 112
online security 77, 177-178
Oprah Winfrey 110
origami 169

P

Paper Denim and Cloth 70
paint 102
Paul Smith 98
Paypal 179
perfume see *fragrances*
personalised
   cards 146, 148
   confetti 150
   photographs and designs 104
   stationery 151-152, 154, 159, 160, 162
   wrapping paper 165
photography 104, 158, 160, 168
   albums 147, 156, 160
   placemats 115
   storage 156, 160
Prada 71, 137
prints 104
privacy 177-178

Q

quilts 102, 109, 118
   see also *bedding, babies* and *children*

R

ribbons 157, 162
Roberto Cavelli 88
rugs 105, 114

S

Sass & Bide 70
scrapbooking 159
secure websites see *online security*
security 3
sewing kits 67
shaving gear 92, 97

shipping 3, 177
shoes
   children 38
   women's 71–72, 88–89
   men's 94–95
silver 115
skincare
   women's 50–65
   men's 92, 97
slippers, women's 77
soaps 40, 50, 53, 55–56
   see also *body-care* and *skincare*
spa products 53
   see also *body-care*
sporting goods 142
Spoylt 88
stationery 75, 145–164
   children's 12, 150–151
   customised 148, 151
   e-stationery 154
storage 112–113, 117–118, 155, 161
   women's accessories 86
strollers 46
Swaravski 143

T

table linen 105, 108–109
tableware 108, 113–114, 116, 118
tea towels 109
Ted Baker 96
throws 104, 108, 111, 113, 118–119
towels 102, 108, 116, 118–119
   see also *children*
toys 6–26, 139, 169
travel accessories 91, 100, 112, 117, 143, 172
   books 123–124

V

Vera Wang 88, 150
Versace 115

W

wallets 92, 96
watches
   men's 96
   women's 69
weddings
   albums 160
   bridal wear 73
   men's apparel 95
   cards 150 see also *stationery*
   personalised art 167
   registry service 118
Willow 70
Witchery 89
women's fashion
   accessories 69–82, 93, 141
   apparel 6, 22, 68–89, 137–138, 140–143
   bridal wear 73
   hosiery 85, 94
   jewellery 79–80, 81
   lingerie 72–73, 77, 82, 88–89, 94, 141
   maternity 71, 73, 85
   plus sizes 85
   shoes 71–72, 83, 89
   sleepwear 70, 76, 81, 87, 88, 94
   slimming apparel 85
   swimwear 72
   thongs (flip flops) 73
Wonderbra 73
wrapping paper 165

XYZ

XO 8
Zid Zid Kids 21

ACKNOWLEDGEMENTS

At the risk of sounding like a teary Oscar-winning actress, there are a few people I would like to thank.

Firstly, my wonderful parents. Your love, support and guidance has been invaluable and I truly couldn't do anything without it. A big thanks to my best friend and sister, Sam, a truthful sounding board and number one cheerleader. Thanks also to my brother-in-law Stu, and a heap of sloppy kisses for Harrison, my incredibly handsome and gifted nephew. The beautiful illustrations in *The Global Shopper* are thanks to the talented Cameron Comer – a great artiste and one of my best friends. To Stepsy, Ant and Erro: thanks for your support and for forgiving me when I failed to return countless phone calls and emails over the past few months.

Thankyou also to the great team at Hardie Grant, especially the amazing Mary Small, and to my editor Martine Lleonart. You both made putting together my first book a pleasure!

Last but not least, a thankyou must go to the web retailers themselves, many of whom provided great support in collating the site reviews.

Nicole has always loved to shop. While her kindergarten buddies liked to paint, Nicole liked to buy paint. While her teenage friends watched Tom Cruise in *Cocktail* over and over again, Nicole was off scouring hidden laneways for imported handbags and shoes. And when it came time for university, Nicole chose the one closest to all major department stores.

All grown up, Nicole still loves to shop but now she goes global. Thanks to the internet, she regularly trawls through the boutiques of London, Paris and New York, all from her Melbourne home. And thanks to the magic of UPS and FedEx, this home is filled with treasured items, many of which can't be bought in Australia.

The birth of her nephew Harrison only fed her obsession – a new being in need of clothing, accessories and toys! She awaits further family developments with a keen eye and a hand on the mouse.